Amazon FBA 2022

A step by step guide to sell on Amazon
with your own private label brand,
ecommerce and dropshipping selling for
beginners

Adam Voegtli

Contents

Introduction

"If you do not find a way to make money while you sleep, you will work until you die." - Warren Buffett.

If you haven't heard of Amazon, you've probably been living under a rock. Amazon is the world's largest online store, and many people use it to sell things online. Jeff Bezos, who is currently worth more than $200 billion, founded the company in the early 1990s as a bookstore.

Fast forward to now: Amazon sells everything imaginable, from toilet paper to complete television sets. Everybody is aware of the excellent products and services they provide. Many people are unaware that they may earn money on Amazon! What the majority of people do not know is that they could be missing out on an incredible opportunity for enterprises or individuals looking to start their own business.

You do not require specialized training. You can have little knowledge and still earn a solid living. It's all about self-education. If you want to differentiate yourself from the competition and earn a genuine profit, the first step is to develop the necessary mindset. Develop a game plan and become familiar with the ins and outs of the business. We're going to examine the company's ins and outs in order to get you started with Amazon FBA.

And we will demonstrate how to do so on a large scale. When we talk about large-scale, we're referring to the millions of dollars that many Amazon FBA sellers earn. It will be challenging, but it will be worthwhile. One critical point, you must ensure that you have the proper strategy in order to generate sales and establish a successful business. This means that you must thoroughly read this book before taking any action.

If you don't understand something in this book, make a point of returning to it as often as possible to gain a deeper understanding. We have invested a great deal of time and effort in presenting you with the greatest knowledge available, but if you do not put in the work, you will not see results. We can provide you with all the information you need, but unless you apply it, reading this book is likely to be a waste of time.

Amazon, or the Everything Store, as it is frequently referred to, wants its vendors to succeed—if they do, Amazon does as well. The lesson is that you should not be disheartened by Amazon's rising vendor base and increased competition. The increase in competition is more than countered by the increase in new opportunities.

Numerous people have amassed fortunes selling through Amazon FBA over the last several years, freeing themselves from the confines of their day jobs and regaining control of their lives. Anyone who hears these success tales wonders if they, too, could accomplish the same thing. However, the subject on everyone's mind is whether Amazon's selling has become too competitive. Keep in mind that it is not too late to start making money on Amazon in 2022.

The reason for this is straightforward: Amazon continues to grow. The worldwide e-commerce company's net sales were 386.06 billion US dollars in the most recent fiscal year (2020), up from 280 billion US dollars in 2019. The corporation achieved $280 billion in revenue in 2019, a 20% increase over the previous year. The previous year, the company expanded by another 31%, and the year before by another 31%. What does this mean for new entrepreneurs?

Even as competition intensifies on Amazon, the company continues to grow at a similar, if not faster, pace, generating an increasing number of chances for new sellers to enter the market. If you follow the recommendations in this book, you, too, may achieve enormous financial success through Amazon product sales.

Before we continue, allow me to quickly explain why I wrote this book. While Amazon has a sizable inventory of hundreds of millions of things, we all know from personal experience that not all of them are great. Books are no different. When I initially started selling on Amazon years ago, I devoured every "How to Sell on Amazon" book available, and I discovered that the majority of them had flaws. The majority of the "fast" or "simple" guides to Amazon FBA were disorganized and unedited.

They lacked a structure that would be beneficial to a new seller. There was also little sign of editing or correction, as the volumes contained several ambiguous interpretations and grammatical faults. Second, the longer and more detailed books ran to hundreds of pages and contained minutiae that might easily overwhelm someone unfamiliar with Amazon FBA. As a complete novice, you are not required to be exposed to or slowed down by this deluge of knowledge. The majority of it will come naturally with experience. What is critical in the beginning is that you master the fundamentals of success. As a result, I set out to develop the finest possible guide for novice sellers—a book that can be read in a few sittings and contains all the information you need to get started.

Now if you're wondering, what does the FBA stand for? It stands for "Fulfillment by Amazon." FBA began as a beta program in 2004. The majority of businesses would agree that it is necessary to have a competitive advantage over other merchants. The Amazon FBA process is straightforward. To begin, you locate a low-cost source and then sell it to customers on Amazon at a markup, leaving you with a profit. Consider Amazon to be comparable to Shopify, with the following exceptions: first, you will be selling your products on Amazon; and second, you will need to ship your products to Amazon's fulfillment center before you can begin fulfilling orders.

So, even if there is an initial cost, there are numerous benefits. For example, you will be promoting your product on a website that already receives a significant amount of free traffic. That is, you will have a greater chance of success at the beginning of selling your products when compared to other ways. Another significant advantage is that there is no need to bother about having a shop because Amazon will act as your storefront.

Amazon contributes to sales growth with its world-class fulfillment and skill in picking, packing, and shipping goods to customers. It has evolved into a revenue-generating platform for third-party sellers and merchants looking to earn passive income by selling things online. Of course, manufacturers and online business owners are not the only ones who may use Amazon to help boost their sales. If you're seeking a true online business opportunity, Amazon has the ability to provide you with a handsome income for the rest of your life. Anyone can sell on Amazon, including college students, people tired of working for others, stay-at-home moms, people looking for extra money, and retirees.

Why do customers pay more on Amazon and you make a hefty profit as a seller?

It's critical to keep in mind that not everyone is completely cost-conscious. Amazon.com caters to everyone who prefers the convenience of shopping online for a product they require, regardless of whether they are Prime members. For some busy professionals, the convenience of having a product brought directly to their homes may outweigh the cost of the item. For a snowed-in family, the additional shipping rate is worth the expense of not having to leave their house during the winter season to purchase an item. Additionally, residents of rural areas would choose to pay an additional price rather than drive an hour each way to buy an item.

If you think about it, the cost and time people spend commuting and purchasing an item are identical to the cost and time they spend with Amazon, but with the added bonus of time savings. People shop on Amazon for the convenience of the shipping service. Certainly, the convenience of having an item delivered directly to their doorsteps makes a difference to customers, to the point where even a small expense overcomes the convenience of having an item.

Selling on Amazon is an excellent option for you to sell things on a well-known network with millions of established buyers. There is a good probability of profiting from the marketplace. Undeniably, selling things on Amazon enables businesses to access a global audience.

Amazon offers the FBA program to alleviate fulfillment challenges for online businesses and to help level the playing field. Amazon merchants have reported profitability, rapid growth in sales, and increased consumer delight as a result of adopting Fulfillment by Amazon. When Amazon sellers joined FBA, in the majority of cases, their sales increased by 20%.

Another reason that Amazon FBA is the best alternative for selling your products online with global exposure is the company's extensive coverage. Additionally, its features and services are quite adaptable. Sellers do not need to reside in the United States to have a shot at business growth. They make the FBA program available to multiple countries through Amazon's global marketplace. Apart from the United States of America, FBA is currently available in the United Kingdom, Canada, France, Italy, Germany, China, Japan, Spain, and Mexico. These countries have fulfillment centers. Surely, Amazon will be able to expand FBA to additional countries in the next few years.

If you're looking for a means to boost your income, change your profession, or improve your lifestyle, focusing only on internet sales may be the answer. Without a doubt, conducting e-commerce on Amazon, an amazing marketplace, can be a good beginning point for selling and launching a business, as well as transitioning from a traditional purchasing and selling model to a new one.

If you're reading this book, you're probably curious to learn more about the subject and to comprehend how this ideal mechanism works, capable of promptly delivering a product you just purchased. I hope this book may assist you and provide a comprehensive review of the subject, as well as serve as a decent introduction to the unique and complex world of online sales, inspiring you to learn more about the new economy.

As a newcomer to Amazon FBA, you may have a number of fair queries, such as: is the Amazon marketplace still viable, or has it become saturated with sellers and products? How much money do I need to get started? Which goods should I concentrate my efforts on? And, once again, is it possible to sell and earn despite Amazon's sales commission? Where do I purchase the products and how are logistics handled? How can I sponsor the product most effectively so that it shows on the first page and is visible to all? How long does it take Amazon to pay me? This book will address all of these concerns!

Using FBA is all about utilizing an already established system to generate passive revenue. Amazon already has a reputation, a client base, and a user-friendly platform that people use on a daily basis. Apart from their online platform, they have a global distribution network. Their packaging and shipping system is established and operates flawlessly on a daily basis. It is simpler for you and me to utilize this system than to attempt to develop our own. This is only one of the several advantages of employing FBA mentioned throughout this book.

I will not sugarcoat any part of Amazon FBA. I'm also not going to try to sell you anything or persuade you to take an additional learning course. There will be resources throughout this book to assist you in continuing your learning experience. All that is required is that you comprehend this step-by-step guide and then put it into action. I completely understand if you're feeling overwhelmed right now. To a new seller, this may seem like a lot.

Prepare your notebook because there will be a lot of information to process. Fortunately, you now have access to what I think to be an excellent resource, and I encourage you to take notes and reread this book twice if required. By the end of this book, you will have acquired all of the knowledge necessary to begin selling your first successful product on Amazon, and you'll be prepared to start earning passive income on your own! Without further ado, let's dive into the specifics of beginning your business using Amazon FBA. Let's get started!

Chapter One

This is Your Game

How Does Amazon FBA Work in 2022? Fulfillment by Amazon.

What exactly is FBA?

For online sellers, FBA stands for "Fulfillment by Amazon," a business model that allows you to use Amazon's massive warehouses to store and transport your products.

How Amazon's FBA Works

Following a few simple steps, you can register your products in your FBA section on Amazon using your regular Amazon selling account. Expanding your business in a cost-effective manner with Amazon's help is as simple as a few clicks. Using Amazon FBA is a simple process.

1.   You send your products to amazon

2.   Amazon stores your products

3.   Customers purchase your products

4.   Amazon picks and packs your product

5.   Amazon ships your product to your customers

Amazon's Role

1. Your merchandise will be shipped to one of Amazon's warehouses, and they'll inform you exactly where to send it.

2. Your merchandise is safe and secure at Amazon's warehouse.

3. Clients order your products, and Amazon takes care of everything, from payment to inventory updates.

4. Amazon takes care of the packaging and shipping of your merchandise for you.

5. As far as customer care goes, Amazon handles the bulk of it, including any returns or refunds.

6. Amazon transfers your sales proceeds into your bank account every two weeks.

Amazon FBA is like having your own warehouse, warehousing staff, and packing crew! To earn money, all you have to do is supply Amazon with the stock, and they'll take care of everything else. Amazon does charge a fee for their FBA service, but the charges are competitive and the postage savings are substantial.

What You Do

- Choose your products: You'll need to do your own research and choose products to offer on Amazon.

- Make sure your inventory is always current: In order to keep your supply levels at a safe level, you need to keep an eye on your inventory and replenish it as necessary.

- Create product listings and successfully sell your goods: Amazon is massive, but you'll still need to write good product descriptions and titles and market your products in order for them to be found by potential customers.

The benefits of Amazon FBA

Some of the perks of Amazon FBA include:

1. You can take full advantage of Amazon's goodwill to your benefit. Countless people throughout the world put their faith in Amazon's products and services. They don't have to wonder if they're going to get their order or not. They also know that if they need to, they may return it. Whether or not they buy from you depends heavily on this.

2. You'll be able to offer lightning-fast service. Faster processing and delivery are two of Amazon's distinctive online ordering features. Consequently, they are able to ship your goods faster than you would be able to.

3. You can get a better Amazon rating and more exposure. Your product will rank higher in search results if you make use of the FBA program. Items listed by total price are those sold by sellers who do not use FBA's services (the price of the product plus shipping costs). If you're an FBA seller,

your items will appear at the top of the search results because they will only be listed according to price.

4. Buy boxes are yours. The Amazon Buy Box is the large "Add to Cart" button that appears on all of Amazon's product pages. Obviously, if you and Amazon are both offering the same goods, Amazon will always have the Buy Box. However, you can still compete with Amazon FBA. Your other product listings are more likely to get the buy box if they use FBA, which is one of Amazon's preferred shipping options.

5. You can offer free shipping by default. Amazon Prime subscribers can enjoy free shipping on all their items. You have a significant advantage over other merchants who are not using Amazon FBA. During the peak of the holiday shopping season, the most affluent customers tend to buy a wide range of goods. With Amazon FBA, you'll be able to win these customers because everyone loves free shipping.

6. There is a huge reduction in your expenses. Your business will be able to focus more on selling more products and increasing revenues thanks to FBA, which takes care of the storage, personnel, and administration for you.

7. Your output will rise, which is good news for you. When you use FBA, you'll be more productive, which is one of its most important advantages. You can focus on growing your business while Amazon handles your customer support, returns, warehousing, packing, and shipping of your products.

8. Running a business from anywhere is possible! With Amazon FBA, you can sell from anywhere on the globe and still have a steady flow of customers coming through. All of your orders will be handled by Amazon 24 hours a day, seven days a week. Customers will contact you less frequently as a result of this. Amazon FBA will take care of

all of your customer support issues. Customers can contact Amazon's customer support instead of you if they have a problem with their order, for example. You won't have to deal with customers face-to-face, which saves you time, tension, and aggravation.

9. The greatest advantage! It's hard to beat Amazon FBA's total user-friendliness. Imagine never needing to handle a product, transmit an order, or deal with a refund ever again!

So, to summarize, Amazon FBA can give you the time you need to focus on other key elements of your business, such as obtaining new stock and raising brand awareness.

The disadvantages of Amazon FBA and possible solutions

1. Amazon FBA costs money. There are storage costs and fulfillment fees charged by Amazon since they are a business with the same goal as yours: to make money. To reduce Amazon storage fees, you'll need to make sure your stock is moving rapidly, and as long as your inventory doesn't just "sit" and you're making sales, further fees won't apply. Also, you'll need to make sure that your products are still lucrative after factoring in the costs associated with FBA. Here is an Amazon fee calculator.
.
https://sellercentral.amazon.com/hz/fba/profitabilitycalculator/index?lang=en_US

1. For Amazon FBA, product preparation can be tricky. By signing up for Amazon FBA, you will have access to all of Amazon's instructions for packing and shipping your products to their facility. You can't afford to make a mistake

with these rules. Incorrectly labeled merchandise will cause delays and annoyance, as well as more work at the warehouse. Following the directions to a T is essential.

2. Your brand does not appear on the product package. Amazon's branding will appear on the package your consumer receives once their order has been shipped by Amazon FBA. Because your brand is not visible on your packaging, it will be more difficult for you to create your reputation through brand awareness. As a result, if brand awareness is a priority for you, you'll need to measure this against the other benefits Amazon FBA provides.

3. You could see an increase in returns: Amazon's "simple returns process" may result in a higher number of returns from customers when you begin using Amazon FBA. You may mitigate this risk by ensuring that your products are of the highest quality so that customers don't feel the need to return them.

For many businesses, these few disadvantages won't outweigh the benefits of Amazon FBA. Of course, your success will also depend on other factors, many of which are down to you, the effort you put in, and the knowledge you have in order to utilize Amazon FBA in the best possible way.

Is Amazon FBA still a good investment strategy?

Amazon FBA is still a viable option in 2022, and we'll explain why in the following paragraphs.

How much money do Amazon sellers make on a regular basis?

Every new Amazon seller wonders, "How much money can I make?" Let's take a look at the current Amazon FBA profit numbers, which show that roughly 85 percent of active sellers are making money on Amazon.

Let's have a look at the monthly sales figures:

- 50% of Amazon sellers make more than $5,000 in sales per month.
- More than a quarter of Amazon merchants make more than $25,000 a month.
- A lifetime sales total of $50,000 or more has been achieved by half of all Amazon sellers
- 19% of Amazon sellers have made more than $1 million in sales over their entire business career.

Monthly sales	Percentage of Amazon sellers
Under $500	17%
$501-$1,000	9%
$1,001 – $5,000	20%
$5,001 – $10,000	13%
$10,001 – $25,000	12%
$25,001 – $50,000	10%
$50,001 – $100,000	5%
$100,001 – $250,000	5%
More than $250,000	6%
I don't know	4%

The revenue figures are impressive, but what about the profit?

There is more to a company's success than just revenue. Assuming you have $1 million in sales but your costs are beyond that, you won't be generating any money. Amazon vendors' profit margins are larger than those of traditional enterprises like brick-and-mortar.

- 60% of Amazon merchants make profit margins of 10% or greater.
- A profit margin of at least 20% is maintained by 36% of Amazon merchants.
- Over the course of their careers, 20% of Amazon sellers have earned more than $100,000.

Since many new sellers begin this business as a side hustle, this isn't bad!

Profit margin	Percentage of Amazon sellers
~1-5%	6%
6-10%	10%
11-15%	13%
16-20%	19%
21-25%	14%
26-50%	19%
51-100%	3%
Not currently profitable	8%
Don't know	8%

While these figures are positive, it's important to remember that 8% of businesses aren't yet profitable, and another 8% aren't sure if they will be in the future.

Is Amazon too crowded for you to succeed?

As you see above, new sellers can still make money on Amazon despite the increased competition over the previous few years. If you're selling in the United States, it's considered the least competitive Amazon marketplace. For every business, there is always going to be competition—which is a good thing because it implies that your items are going to have a market. As many as 600,000 new merchants are expected to join Amazon this year.

That may seem overwhelming, but keep in mind that Amazon's market share is increasing every month, quarter, and year, depending on how you look at it. Although more vendors may increase competition, you won't be taking sales from each other but rather expanding your client base. If you are a new seller, make sure

It is critical that you conduct thorough research before deciding on a product to sell. Make sure you do your homework before launching an e-commerce or Amazon business.

Every business can benefit from Amazon FBA.

Amazon FBA is used by millions of e-commerce entrepreneurs, but it's not going to be appropriate for every business. While it may not be ideal for everyone, it is an excellent alternative for Amazon sellers who want to grow their business and avoid becoming mired down in the tedious chore of fulfilling orders, especially if they're trapped between a small business and a full-time operation. Amazon's FBA program might be a lucrative and profitable business opportunity.

In order to make an informed decision about whether or not to join Amazon, you'll need to do your due diligence and understand Amazon's laws and restrictions, as well as know your customers—your target market. In the end, how well Amazon FBA works for you will be determined by the products you sell and the goals you set for your company. There are many benefits to outsourcing some of the responsibilities connected with running an online business to Amazon, but you must ensure that the benefits outweigh the additional costs.

What do you need to perform well on Amazon?

Your potential profits are clear, but how much does it cost to get started on Amazon? Investing in something will necessitate both a financial and time commitment.

Money

"How much money should I begin with?" is one of the most frequently asked questions by prospective Amazon sellers. While 58% of Amazon sellers started with $5,000 or more, 28% started with $1,000 or less, and 18% started with just $500! You'll need extra money if you want to start your own private-label brand. You can start making money right away if you choose retail arbitrage or wholesale as your starting point.

How did sellers raise money for their businesses?

58 percent of Amazon sellers used their own or borrowed money to get started. When starting off, I propose bootstrapping (starting with a small amount of money and reinvesting it) or personal savings if you don't have much. New sellers should avoid using credit cards or loans since they may have difficulty repaying their debts if they purchase poor inventory.

Some 17 percent of vendors borrowed money from a family member, while about 12 percent acquired some form of business loan to get started.

How long did it take for them to achieve profitability?

When compared to a conventional small business, Amazon sellers are able to make money significantly more quickly. Despite the fact that it may take more than two years to make a profit, 20% of Amazon sellers reported making a profit in less than three months. It's not a "get rich quick" scam, but it is possible to start making money right away on Amazon. This isn't always the case, however. It may take some time for new sellers to start making money, especially if they're just getting started. According to 17 percent of vendors, they made a profit in 3-6 months, while 16 percent said it took them around a year or more. During the early stages of a private-label product's lifecycle, this is frequent. For their listings to get off to a good start, sellers are pouring money into marketing and advertising.

Time

To succeed on Amazon, you must put in the time it takes to succeed. Just like 54% of other Amazon sellers have done, you can launch your first product in just three months if you're consistent in your efforts. 31% of them were up and running within six weeks or less! You don't have to get up and running right away. More than a third of Amazon merchants required six months to a year to get up and running. Your comfort level is the only thing that matters.

How many hours a week do sellers devote to their businesses, on average?

Managing your business after it's up and running is a necessary part of owning a business. If you use FBA to handle all order logistics, as 39% of sellers do, you could be working on your business for as little as 10 hours per week. At first, you'll likely devote more time to your project. 16% of Amazon sellers work between 21 and 30 hours per week, while 17% work more than 40 hours per week. The amount of time you devote to your business depends on your goals.

Is Amazon FBA worth the time and money?

Yes, Amazon is competitive. For the most part, it isn't something you can just start and forget about, despite what many people think. An Amazon FBA business demands patience, perseverance, and hard effort to succeed. What about the cost? As far as we are concerned, we say yes. We believe that selling on Amazon has significantly more advantages than disadvantages. Does Amazon guarantee that every entrepreneur who creates a product will succeed? Assuming that you put in the effort and keep learning from your failures, you will be a successful Amazon seller in the long run.

It's simple enough for the average person to accomplish. Why don't you?

Chapter Two

Forming Your business and Preparing to Sell

Do Amazon sellers require a limited liability company?

Amazon sellers, like other online entrepreneurs, should think about the impact their business structure has on their professional and personal lives. Income tax responsibilities, ongoing business compliance needs, and legal and financial liability of the company owner are all influenced by the business entity type chosen.

To answer your question, "Do Amazon Sellers Need an LLC?", no. However, you will find plenty of reasons to register your business as an LLC

Consider the benefits of functioning as a company entity other than a general partnership or a sole proprietorship, even if Amazon doesn't appear to demand it. There are many advantages to using the Limited Liability Company (LLC) form of company for small businesses, including lower costs and less complexity than a corporation. I strongly advise anyone contemplating a company entity change to get the advice of an attorney and tax counsel first. In the meantime, I'd like to provide you with the following information:

1. What is a Limited Liability Company?

2. Why might Amazon sellers benefit from setting up an LLC?

3. What are the processes involved in founding an LLC?

What is an LLC?

An LLC is a legal entity that isn't a corporation.

A limited liability company is a separate legal entity that is registered with the state. It is distinct from its owners, unlike a single owner or general partnership. Most of the time, owners (sometimes referred to as "members") are not held responsible for the company's legal troubles or debts. There are many similarities between corporations and LLCs (such as electing a board of directors and holding shareholder meetings), but an LLC does not have to adhere to many corporate procedures (such as requiring substantial corporate records).

For Amazon sellers, LLCs have many benefits.

The LLC structure reduces the personal liability of the business owner.

If you own a sole proprietorship or a partnership, you are the same legal entity. The owners' personal assets (such as their homes, cars, retirement funds, etc.) are in danger if someone sues the firm or the business fails to pay its debts if an Amazon seller runs as either of those entities. Although Amazon sellers can insulate themselves from the legal and financial liabilities of their firm by forming an LLC, the business is regarded as a separate legal entity from their owners.

Flexibility in Income Taxes Is Provided by the LLC Structure

Amazon sellers can pick from two federal income tax treatment options when they form an LLC for federal tax purposes.

1. A partnership or sole proprietor receives the same tax status under pass-through taxes.

2. Corporate taxation

3. S Corporation election

If the Amazon seller's LLC chooses the same federal income tax treatment, most states will follow suit. Check with the Secretary of State's office to see if there are any additional fees for the LLC. As an example, in some states, LLCs, partnerships, and corporations are subject to a franchise tax. Several factors will influence which approach is the most cost-effective. Before making a decision, I recommend consulting an accountant or tax specialist.

LLC Pass-Through Taxation

Choosing this option allows an Amazon seller to transfer the LLC's profits and losses onto their own personal tax returns. Instead of the LLC paying taxes on its own, each member of the LLC pays taxes based on their individual tax rates and the proportion of the LLC they possess. The members of an LLC are self-employed and must pay their full Social Security and Medicare tax requirements on the LLC's taxable income.

Corporate Taxation for LLCs

Tax returns will be filed and income tax paid on behalf of the Amazon seller's LLC if it is treated as a separate legal entity. "Double taxation" is a term you may have heard before if you choose this method of taxation. Members of an LLC are taxed at the corporate rate when they get wages from the LLC and then at the individual tax rates when they file their personal tax returns.

S Corporation Election

In some cases, the S Corp election may be a fair compromise between the first two alternatives for Amazon sellers who incorporate an LLC. Individual members of an LLC can elect to be taxed as an S Corporation, which means that all business income passes through to their individual tax returns, but only self-employment taxes (Self-Sufficiency Insurance and Medicare) apply to members' salaries and earnings. Self-employment taxes are not levied on other business revenues that are distributed to shareholders as dividends. This prevents corporate double taxation and reduces the personal tax burden of the company's founders and shareholders.

Flexibility in management is a benefit of the LLC structure.

Member-managed LLCs and manager-managed LLCs exist. As a result, members have a wide range of options as to whom they trust to make day-to-day business decisions. In most states, an LLC is assumed to be administered by its members unless the formation documents explicitly declare otherwise. Member-owned LLCs allow the owners to run the firm and make day-to-day decision-making for the company.

If an LLC is managed by a manager, it means that the members have designated or hired someone (or more than one person) to carry out such duties. In some cases, the LLC's manager may also be a shareholder. In either situation, the Amazon seller's LLC operating agreement should specify the particular tasks and authority of the LLC members and managers. If everyone is on the same page, there will be no confusion regarding who is responsible for operating the company.

The LLC's business compliance requirements are quite straightforward.

The LLC form, when compared to other business entity types, offers the most simplicity after operating as a single proprietor or partnership. In most states, LLCs are required to comply with a few rules, although they are far fewer in number than the responsibilities that corporations have. When incorporating an LLC, Amazon resellers face fewer paperwork requirements as well as fewer filings and formalities on a regular basis.

Forming an LLC for Amazon Sellers

In order to form an LLC, there are a few essential steps:

1. Pick a name for your company.

2. Designate a Registrar of Deeds.

3. Form a company in the state.

4. Obtain a tax identification number (Federal Tax ID Number.)

5. The LLC Operating Agreement should be written.

6. Acquire the necessary licenses and permits for your Amazon business (including a sales tax permit).

7. You need to open a business bank account.

8. Maintain a clean business record by adhering to all applicable state laws and regulations.

Vendors on Amazon and Sales Tax

A major hurdle for Amazon sellers, regardless of their business structure, is dealing with state sales tax. Budget-conscious governments in need of income have started to tighten up on merchants who weren't collecting and remitting sales tax in the past. For online purchases, it's not always clear which state's sales tax must be paid. Does a vendor have to pay sales tax to the state where they are incorporated?

Or does the tax get collected in the state where the product was sold and shipped? The state in which the fulfillment warehouse is located determines whether or not sales tax is owed by the company. It is possible that any state where Amazon conducts business and sells its items may require Amazon merchants to apply for international qualification in order to collect and remit sales tax.

An experienced tax accountant or attorney can help you navigate this complex scenario.

GS1 Barcodes are required by the most prominent retailers. If you are listing your products on the internet, then you need a GS1 barcode from the United States. You must have an authentic barcode in order to sell on the major online marketplaces. GS1 is the world's barcode authority.

• A GTIN (Global Trade Item Number) is still used to identify a product even when the barcode is not scanned at online checkout as it is at the cash register.

• There's nothing better than the fact that GS1 barcodes are acknowledged worldwide.

- When you post your merchandise on a retailer's website, you'll have the same barcode to list it on another retailer's website and in retail stores.

Before allowing you to sell on their site, retailers often check your barcodes in the GS1 database. Your account may be banned or you may be required to rebrand your products if your business is not identified as the brand owner of that barcode in the system. You'll have to spend time and resources on both! Invest in the future of your business by obtaining a GS1 Company Prefix or a GS1 GTIN for your barcodes. A GS1 GTIN is a single barcode, whereas a GS1 Company Prefix allows you to license an entire block of barcodes at once. To get GS1 barcodes for your company please head to https://www.gs1us.org/

Improved search results can be achieved by using GS1 Barcodes. Companies such as Google and Bing are more likely to link your merchandise to their product catalog if it has a barcode with accurate product data.

Number of items needing a barcode/GTIN**	Initial fee	Annual renewal fee
1 GS1 US GTIN	$30	NONE
10	$250	$50
100	$750	$150
1,000	$2,500	$500
10,000	$6,500	$1,300
100,000	$10,500	$2,100
NDC/NHRIC Company Prefix	$2,100	$2,100

Product barcodes are mandated by FBA.

Barcodes are used to identify and monitor merchandise throughout the fulfillment process by Amazon's fulfillment service. A barcode is required for each item that you deliver to an Amazon fulfillment facility. Products can be identified using one of three types of barcodes:

• UPC, EAN, JAN, and ISBN are examples of valid barcodes

• Barcodes for Amazon products (such as FNSKU)

• Authentic code for transparency. Only the brand owner may be required to assist in the prevention of counterfeiting.

If your company has been recognized in the Amazon Brand Registry but you do not have a producer barcode for your merchandise, you can ask for a GTIN exemption. It is important to note that if your brand has been accepted into the Amazon Brand Registry but you do not have a manufacturer barcode for your items, you can request an exemption from the GTIN requirement.

Manufacturer barcodes

Without changing your barcode option, Amazon will utilize the factory barcode to track qualified stock through the fulfillment process by default, unless you specify otherwise. When more than one vendor has stock with the same producer barcode, Amazon may complete orders with inventory from the seller who is closest to the consumer, resulting in a faster delivery time for them. If your merchandise is not qualified for virtual tracking using the manufacturer's barcode, an Amazon barcode will be required in addition to the manufacturer's barcode. More information on virtual tracking, as well as product eligibility requirements, may be found at Using Amazon virtual tracking.

While it is possible that your product does not fulfill the standards for virtual-tracking qualification, you may be eligible for an exemption from the requirement to utilize the producer barcode by submitting an application with Amazon Brand Registry and registering your ASIN (Amazon Standard Identification Number) in the program. Non-brand-registered vendors would be required to attach Amazon barcodes to ineligible products in order to sell them on Amazon.

Note: If you are a supplier or a brand owner who wants to display barcodes directly on package design, you can apply for a UPC barcode that is compliant with the Global Standards Institute (GS1) standard.

Amazon barcodes

According to the guidelines, Amazon barcodes must be affixed to any products that are not being tracked by the company's barcode. The following are examples of such products:

• Products that are no longer packaged in their original containers or boxes

• Products that do not contain a scannable UPC, EAN, JAN, or ISBN barcode are referred to as non-scannable products. Products that are not for sale and dangerous items

• Expiration dates are attached to products.

• Products that are consumed or applied topically

• media-related products

• Products for children or infants are available.

You have the option of printing Amazon barcodes and applying them to your goods yourself, or you can have Amazon print and attach them for you for a fee based on the number of items you sell. Use an Amazon barcode to track and trace, and the FBA Label Service is a good place to start for more details.

Bear in mind that Amazon's barcode can also be used to track things that require supplementary wrappings, such as bagging or bubble wrap. The ready item, on the other hand, will require labeling. Continue reading "Labeled products before sending or replenishing inventory" for more details.

Transparency, authenticity codes

In order to protect companies and buyers against counterfeit goods, transparency codes are labels that are placed on individual items. Transparency codes are distinguished by the presence of the Transparency "T" emblem, and they must not be covered or obscured by any other marking. Transparency has further information and a sample sticker that you may download.

Note: Virtual monitoring is available for products that have been enrolled in the Transparency program, with the exception of products in the Toys & Games and Baby Products categories, as well as dangerous goods and products that have an expiration date. Amazon reserves the right to modify the areas qualifying for transparency at any time. More information can be found at Transparency 2D barcode requirements.

The step-by-step process of setting up your Amazon Seller Central Account

Now we are going to discuss setting up your Amazon Seller Central account step-by-step. If you're in the USA, Canada, Europe, Australia, or if you're on any of the approved country lists, this guide will work for you. Obviously, one of the cool things about Amazon FBA and Amazon.com is that all you need is a laptop from anywhere around the world, and you can start selling and building an Amazon FBA business.

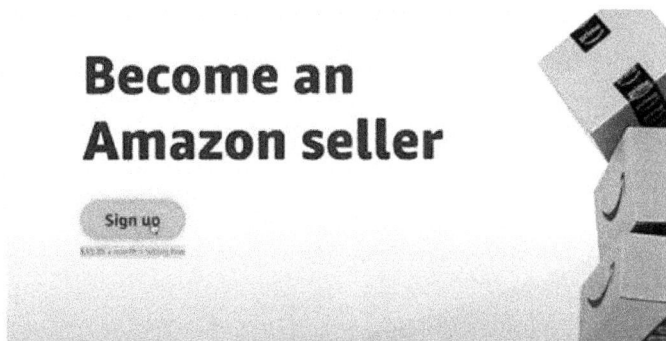

Go to Google and all you have to do is go ahead and type in "Amazon Seller Central." Click "Register Now". This is going to take you to the signup page. You can go ahead and sign up. It's $39.99 a month plus selling fees. The professional account is $39.99 a month, plus selling fees that are just like the referral fees and the FBA fees that Amazon takes.

Individual accounts are cheaper; it's just a dollar per product you sell, but if you plan on selling 40 products per month, obviously, $39.99 makes sense for you and it actually unlocks Amazon PPC, which is just Amazon advertising, and you're going to want to use this for your business.

amazon seller central

Get started selling on
Amazon

Email (phone for mobile accounts)

Password   Forgot your password?

Next

Keep me signed in. Details ▾

New to Amazon?

Create your Amazon account

© 1996-2020, Amazon.com, Inc. or its affiliates

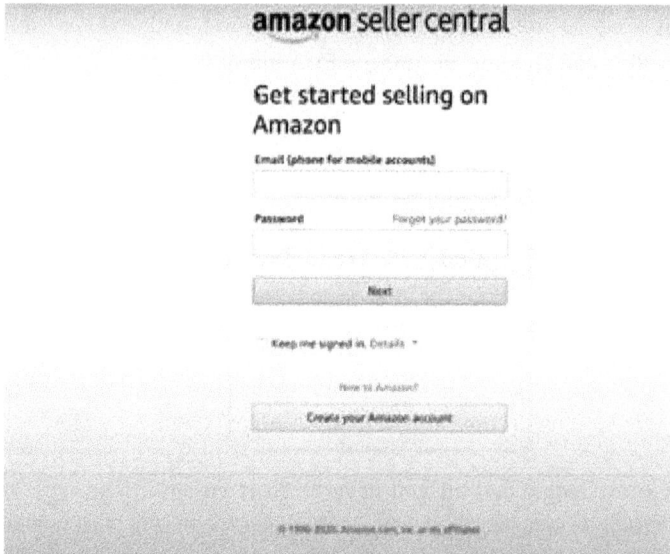

If you want to set up your individual account, you can. However we highly recommend signing up for a professional account. Now, sign up for the $39.99/month professional account. The good news is after paying the initial $39.99 you won't have any charges until you have stock in the warehouse and you're ready to sell, so there's no risk here.

If you have an Amazon Prime account already, you can actually just use that email and password. I don't suggest doing this. I suggest you create your own Amazon account using your business email if you have one. If not, just quickly go and create a Gmail account with your business name or your potential business name. That way, you guys can separate it once you grow and grow and grow. You're going to get a ton of emails from customer inquiries and just Amazon updates, so you want to keep that separate.

Let's hit "Create your Amazon account" right here, so you are going to put in your full name. For example, James Cameron. Once you hit next, it'll ask you to verify your email; simply go to your email and enter the one time password; once you do that, you are finally in, and this is where you will begin registering for your account.

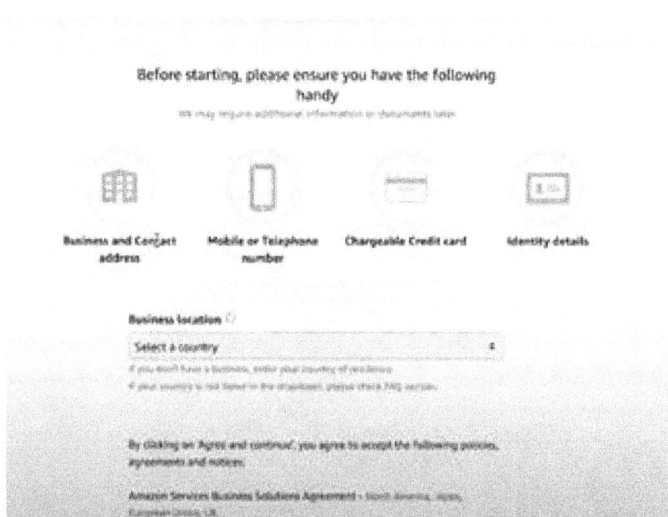

You can see Amazon saying that you need all this information before you proceed, so let's talk about each one real quick. Make sure you have the right documents. So the first one is the business and contact address. This is your location, your address, so what you're going to want to use here if you have a business is your business address.

Now the next question you probably have is, "Should I have a business or not when starting an Amazon account?" I suggest you have an LLC or a corporation, depending on your country. In the USA, an LLC is your best option. You can get one in a day. You can use a service and pay around $100 to $150 to get this set up quickly, or you can go to your state's treasurer page and set it up that way. It just takes a little longer because you have to fill out all the forms. You can use Wyoming registered agent.net to start your LLC.

It's $50 a year to set up your own LLC in Wyoming. There are some cool perks to setting up a Wyoming LLC. For example, it can help with taxes and things like that. It's easier for you to just get it done in your state. I just like this because you can do it on your own in 15 minutes and get a unique address in Wyoming for your business. If you're from Canada or the UK, a corporation is probably your best bet. The next one is a mobile or telephone number. You should have a telephone number or a mobile phone.

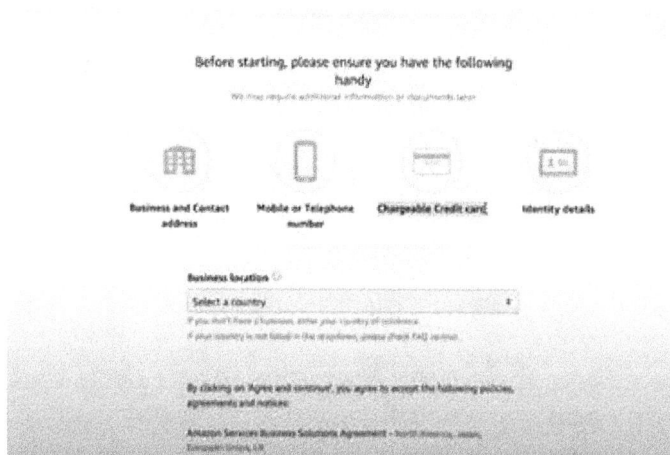

The next is a chargeable credit card, so this one's actually very important. If you have a business credit card, that's perfect.

You have to use a credit card with your business's name on it if registering with an LLC. This is very, very important to make sure you don't get suspended for unnecessary reasons. Make sure to use chargeable credit. You can always change your card later, so let's say you start with a personal credit card, you can go ahead and get it on file and change it to your business credit card later.

Next are identity details, so they're going to ask for your driver's license or passport. Either one works here, and you most likely need a bank statement or a utility bill. It just depends on the account, and probably depends on the location.

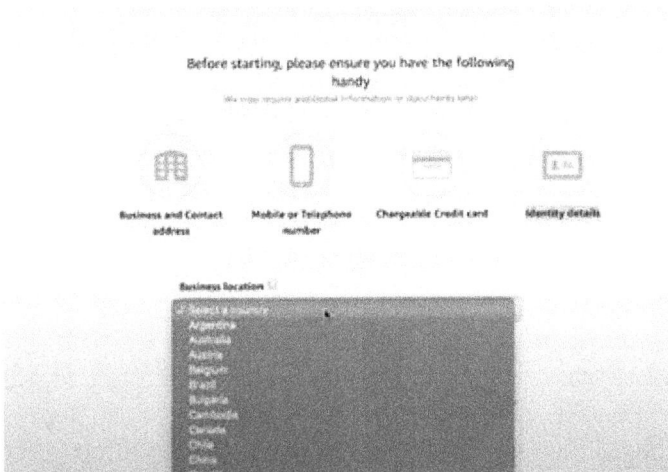

You are going to go ahead and select a business location, so for you, it'd be the United States. Next, it's going to introduce a business type for the US. It might be a little different depending on your location, but here you are going to select a privately owned business if you have an LLC. Ideally, your company should be an LLC.

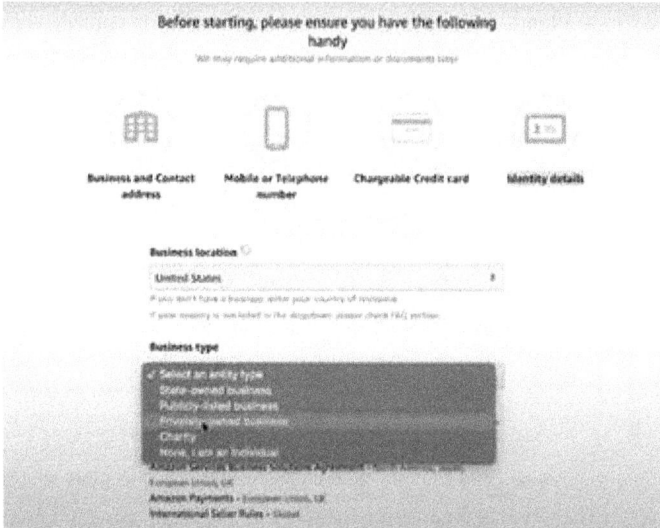

Make sure you put LLC in the right category here. Once you put that in here, it's going to ask you for that business name. Type in the name of your business.

Then go ahead and move on here.

So on the next page, the first thing it's going to ask you is the company registration number.

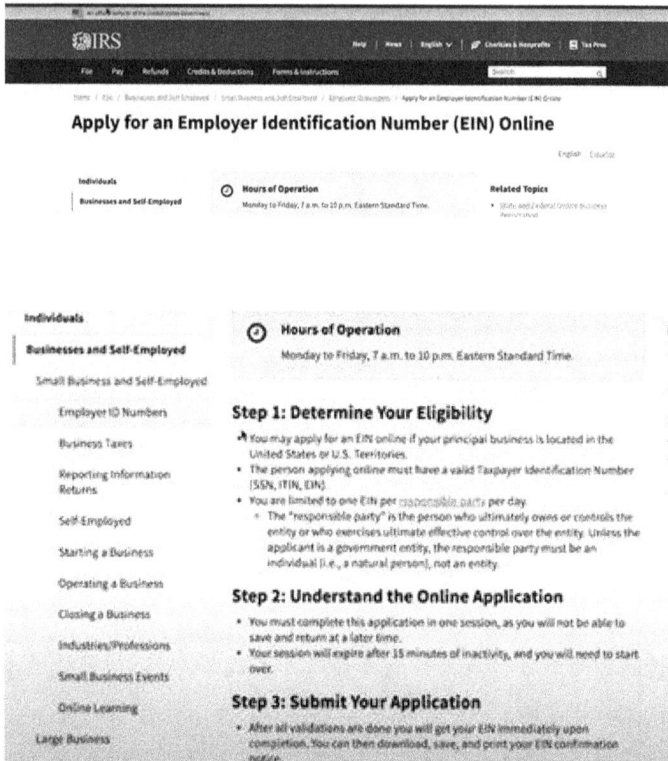

Apply for an Employer Identification Number (EIN) Online

Step 1: Determine Your Eligibility

Step 2: Understand the Online Application

Step 3: Submit Your Application

This is different for different types of businesses and different types of countries. For an LLC, it's an Employer Identification Number (EIN). You can get your EIN by visiting www.irs.go

You'll be able to get it in a couple of minutes, all you do is apply online now, put in your LLC information, and out pops an EIN, which is pretty much like a social security number for your LLC here in the states.

Business Information for **Camron James LLC**

Company registration number

Jurisdiction of business

Registered business address

(i) We will validate this address by sending you a postcard containing a verification code. To avoid any delays please enter your address in English characters only.

Address Line 1	Address Line 2
City / Town	State / Region
United States	ZIP / Postal code

The next part is the jurisdiction of the business. So you put your state here wherever it is formed. This will be in what ever state you decided on registering your business in. And then put in your business address.

Receive PIN through
○ SMS   Call
Phone number for verification

+1 201 555 0125
Example: +81 201 266 1000

SMS verification language

| English | Send SMS |

Primary contact person

| First name | Middle name(s) | Last name |

Enter your complete name, as it appears on the passport or ID

Then finally, you put in your phone number, and then you go ahead and verify that through a text message or a call. It will give you another one-time code for your phone to make sure that it is a real phone number, and then as the primary contact person, you'll just put in your real name right here, so once you enter your code, everything is approved.

This is the next page, and it will ask you for your personal information. First, the country of citizenship. Choose the United States. Go ahead and put your date of birth here. Next is proof of identity. You can use a passport or your driver's license.

Personal Information for

Country of citizenship

United States

Country of birth   Date of birth

United States   Day   Month   Year

Proof of Identity   Date of expiry

Passport . number   Day   Month   Year

Country of Issue

Select country

Residential address

+ Add another address

Mobile number

+ Add a new mobile number

Go ahead and put in whatever you have there and the date of an expert as well as the country of the issue, so choose the United States. Next is the residential address, so put your business address here. If you want to put in your residential address, then go ahead and just hit "add another address." You can add as many phone numbers as you want here.

Residential address

+ Add another address

Mobile number

+ Add a new mobile number

is a beneficial owner of the business
is a legal representative of the business

I have added all the Beneficial Owners of the Business.
Yes   No

Previous   Save

Next, it's asking you who is the beneficial owner of the business or just a legal representative of the business, so you are going to put yourself as the owner right here. If you have business partners, add them here. All done. Go down here and click Save.

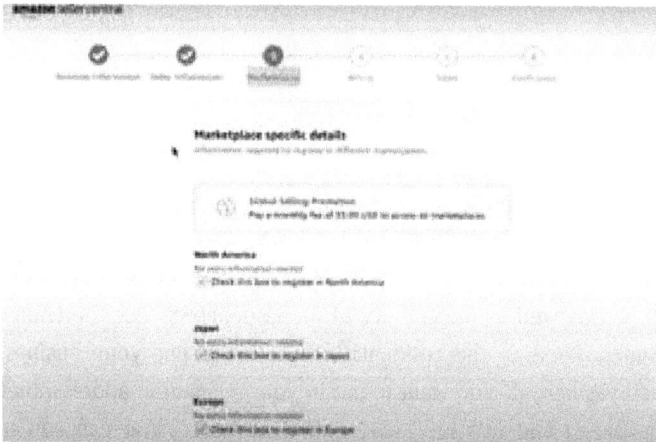

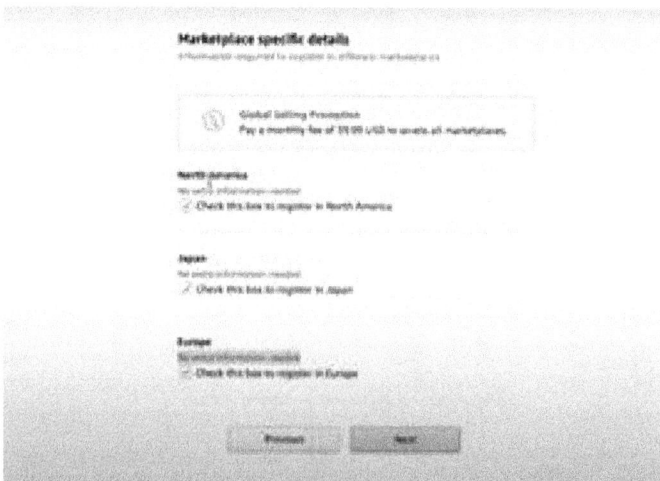

Next, it's going to take you to the market places. Hopefully, this will be a perk for everybody. For example, Canadians, Australians, and Europeans. But here in the USA, they're giving you the option to set up all the way across North America, which gives you access to selling in Mexico and Canada, which is great. It's not necessary, but it's a cool kind of perk once you're ready and once you're ready to take your Amazon business to the next step.

You will have access to Japan and the European countries with no extra information needed. Check these boxes. It's not going to hurt you. Obviously, you are not going to sell there right away, but you might as well have it all set up and ready to go once you get to that point in your business. Go ahead and hit Next.

So next up is billing, so ideally put in your business credit card here, but if you don't have one yet, that's okay, put in your personal credit card and you can always change this information later. You have to start somewhere, as long as it's not a debit card because they will suspend your account and they will not tell you why.

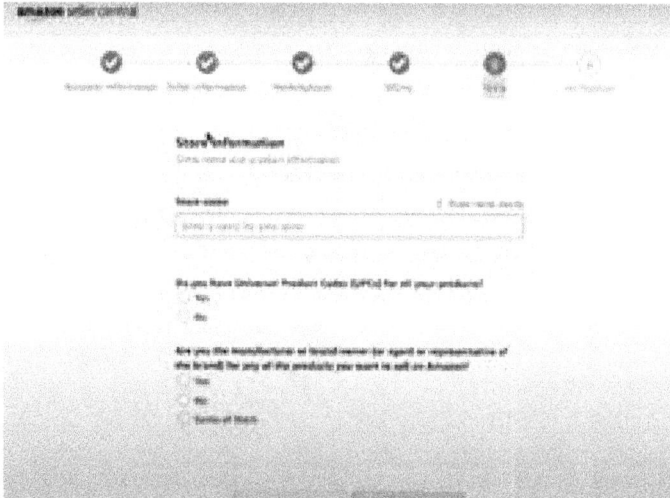

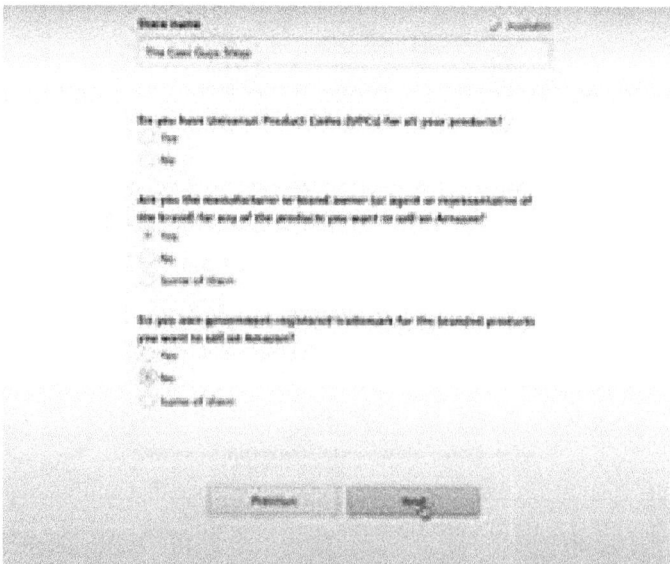

So the next page is the store page. What they want here is a store name for your business. The cool thing is that it doesn't have to be your business name. It could be anything you want. So put here a very generic name that can cover the basics of all types of brands. For example, if you put a name like Sports Plus, well, you're going to have to stick with Sports because your store name has the word Sports in it.

So for this one, let's put "the cool guy's shop" or something like that. Amazon is going to tell you if this is available or not, and if it's not, you've just got to change your name, obviously. If you have a physical store, you will almost certainly have a UPC, so hit yes.

But if you're just starting out and haven't got your product figured out yet, then choose no. Next is either a manufacturer or a brand owner for any of the products you want to sell on Amazon. If you're a private label, you're going to hit "yes" here.

Do you own a government-registered trademark for the brand-new products you want to sell? If you had a product that was already trademarked, then you would hit "yes" here. You're going to hit no. If you're just starting out with the private label, then hit next.

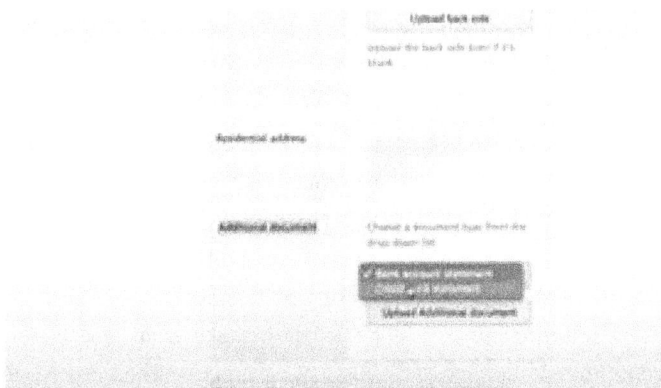

So the last and final step is probably the most tricky and most important to get approved on time for your Amazon account and is the identity verification step. It's got all our information right here. Go ahead and upload your identity document, whether you chose a passport or a driver's license. Next is your address. Make sure you upload the correct information.

Where it gets tricky is with additional documents. You can choose a bank account statement or you can choose your credit card statement. You can upload your bank statement for your business. When you get an LLC, you can take all your documents to a local bank and get a business bank account set up. You can even do it online in some states, and it's pretty easy to do. Make sure you do this in your own home country.

Make sure the document is in good condition. Make sure it's all visible. Make sure it's not in a foreign language because if it's in a foreign language, they could decline it, so go ahead and get it translated to English if you can hire a translator, or hopefully, your bank will provide it in English for you, then update it there so you can add bank account statements or credit card statements. Choose whatever works best for you.

Just make sure the document is from an established bank, like Chase or Bank of America. Don't try to use your small little credit union or things that would be less likely to get accepted nationwide. It's the same thing with your credit cards. Add your Chase cards, your Capital, and your Discover cards. Use the big national brands over the smaller credit card companies.

Finally, double-check all of your business address and business name information. You don't want to make a mistake that is going to hold up the whole application process. Then finally, go ahead and hit submit.

So, a couple of things to note after using this submit button is that they could decline or ask for more information. They do this on about 1 to 5% of the accounts anyway. So don't be shocked or upset if they do this to you. Just make sure you're following up with an email and giving them all the documents, they want with the most information possible. You can try to tap into your lawyer's side when you're writing back to them. Be as detailed as possible. Provide all of the information in a step-by-step fashion. That way, they don't second-guess themselves and decline your application.

Otherwise, it could just take a couple of weeks to get approved. That's why it's important to go ahead and do this while you're doing product research or before you do product research to get this setup going just in case there are any hiccups at all. Usually, there are no hiccups, but if there are, don't panic. I hope that this step-by-step guide helped you out. Follow the steps. Just make sure you're doing everything to the tee to make sure you get approved as fast as possible.

Chapter Three

Finding Your Perfect Product

Product research is important. There are numerous instances where new Amazon sellers didn't do product research and picked products that didn't sell well. As a result, they suffered losses and had to quit Amazon FBA. As such it's important to understand what makes for a great product and then we can get into finding the product you want to sell.

Perfect product criteria

The Good & The Bad	GOOD PRODUCTS	BAD PRODUCTS
	• Usually cheap to ship, depending on the margins	• Expensive to ship
	• Profit margins of 30%+ percent (after Amazon fees)	• Profit margins below 30% percent (after Amazon fees)
	• Low to medium competition	• High competition & hard to differentiate products
	• Main keyword has over 1,500 searches per month (important)	• Glass (if it's your **first or second** product)
	• Potential to create bundles and develop brand	• Potential to create bundles and develop brand
	• Priced between $15 to $75	• Seasonal (ex. Halloween products)

Before we discuss product research approaches, it's critical to discuss what makes a good product. We're going to explore the factors involved in selecting a quality product. On the left, you'll see what goes into making a good product; on the right, you'll see what goes into making a bad one. Bear in mind that not every single thing you sell must meet every single one of these criteria. Your primary concerns, I would argue, are profit margins and competition, specifically the number of identical products available. For-profit margins, we want to ensure that the product we're considering has at least 30% profit margins after Amazon's fees.

When I mention Amazon fees, I'm referring to the commission that Amazon takes on each and every good that you sell. Additionally, there are shipping, pick-up, and delivery expenses. By pick and pack fees, I mean the amount charged by Amazon for physically obtaining the product, picking it up from the warehouse, and then shipping it.

Profit margins of 30% after Amazon fees are arguably the most crucial criterion to follow. Secondly, I would prioritize shipping. The lighter products will be less expensive to market, as the majority of your products will come from China or India. Your products are manufactured in these countries. They make their way to the Amazon warehouse. Then they will be sent directly to the customer from the Amazon warehouse. Therefore, if you're selling a heavier item, it's going to be quite pricey. Not only will it be more expensive to ship it from another country to America, but it will also be more expensive for Amazon to distribute it to the consumer. So, it is normally preferable to have a lighter product.

However, once again, it depends on the profit margins. If the product is slightly heavier and the profit margins are higher, say

40% or 50%, then it may make sense to move on with that product. However, this also depends on the other requirements. Additionally, you want to ensure that the product faces little to moderate competition. If you have a product with a high-profit margin but a lot of competitors, it's usually not a good idea to sell it because you'll be competing directly with them. Not just for sales, but also for advertisements. Therefore, advertising your goods on Amazon will be more expensive if there is more competition to sell those things on Amazon.

Additionally, the keyword will be important. When we're on the lookout for a product, and this is something we'll discuss further within Helium 10, or Jungle Scout, or whatever software you're using, you want to ensure that the primary keyword receives at least 1500 monthly searches. That is critical. However, you can have something with a thousand monthly searches. And if the price is exceptionally low and there is little competition, it may make sense to sell those products.

Similarly, some products receive thousands of monthly searches but have profit margins of 60 to 50%. Circumstances like these make sense for selling the product. This is also something that will be critical in the future when it comes to developing your brand.

The possibility of creating bundles. In an ideal world, you would deliver a new product every quarter. It does not have to be a completely new product each time. It might literally be the same product that you sold at your initial launch. However, it can be packaged with another product.

Assume I'm selling cell phones and would like to create a new package. I could just sell headphones to go with my phone, which would be a completely new product. I'll even go a step beyond. I may sell phones, headphones, and a case for a total of three things. Selling bundles is an excellent way to earn extra money and set yourself apart from your competitors. And finally, for a good product, it should be priced between $15 and $75.

Find The Right Price

IMPULSE BUYING RANGE

- Products selling between $15-$75 fall in the impulse buying decision range.
  - At this range, a customer wouldn't be afraid to make a quick purchase because it's inexpensive.

HOW PRICE APPLIES TO SOURCING

- A product with a selling price of about $25 can be easily sourced from China for about $5. For sourcing 500 products it would require about $5000.
  - A product selling for $100 can cost $12,500 (Higher initial cost)

The reason why this price should be around this level is that this is the point at which individuals make impulse purchases, usually over seventy-five dollars. You will notice this clearly when the level of sales fluctuates. However, we want customers who will purchase again and are comfortable purchasing a product in this category. Additionally, this comes into play because if you have a product that sells for $100, it will cost an exorbitant amount of money to source it from a manufacturer. Keep that in mind. The more expensive a product is on Amazon, the more expensive it will be for you to manufacture that product.

10+ Sales Per Day

AIM FOR 10+ UNITS PER DAY

- Let's say you find a product that sells for $30 and sells 10 units per day. The total profit after the Amazon FBA fees, shipping, promotions, etc is $10

The **revenue** you gross per month is $30 * 10 units * 30 days = $9000.

On average this mean you get a profit of $10 * 10 units (per day) * 30 days (month) = $3000 per month in **profits**

This means the better the average sales per day, the more profits.

Now let's discuss the daily sales volume for this item. Generally, I prefer to find an item that will sell at least ten units every day. Consider the following hypothetical scenario: assume we have a product that sells for thirty dollars on Amazon and sells ten units every day, but also profits. Ten bucks for each unit sold. Ten units are sold each day. By selling for $30 on Amazon, you can expect to earn $900 every month. This is now revenue.

Now, we also want to ensure that this product is profitable. So when we find our product later in the chapter we're also going to estimate profitability using a tool on amazon as well. Generally, we're looking for a product with a profit margin of 30-40%. This will help ensure that you can cover marketing costs with amazon PPC and still make money.

Lightweight Product

IDEAL WEIGHT

- Ideally, your first product should be relatively cheap to ship. Try to keep it under 3 pounds.
  - However, if you're confident with a heavier product that has very high margins, low competition, and isn't bulky it could be worth it.

GLASSWARE IS HIGH-RISK

- Stay away from glassware until you are able to take on the high-risk. This should not be your first, second, or even third product.
  - I know first hand that selling glassware is high-risk, high-reward. You can take extreme losses if things go bad.
  - Glass is heavy and frequently breaks during shipping

That is why having items that sell numerous times every day is critical. Maintain an optimal weight of roughly three pounds. If you discover a product that is heavier, ensure that you can compensate with greater margins or fewer competitors. You do not have to adhere to the optimal weight, but if selling something somewhat heavier, (say six pounds) makes sense and there are only two or three competitors selling it, and it generates, say, fifteen thousand dollars per month in income, then it could be a solid product.

Now I'd want to discuss something to avoid. Trust me, avoid glassware. The reason you want to avoid it is that glass can, of course, break. It will travel a considerable distance between your manufacturer and the Amazon warehouse, and subsequently to the consumer. Throughout that time period, there are several opportunities for glass to break. Not only that, but glass is typically heavier. That is why I advise against it. It simply creates a slew of complications. Believe me, I've experienced it with the test product. Avoid it at all costs.

Year-Around Demand

NO SEASONAL PRODUCTS

- Yes, seasonal items can be extremely lucrative. However, if you're looking for your first product then it's best to sell something that is in demand all year.

- Once you have an established business with several products and great cash flow, then I recommend pursuing seasonal items.

- Determine the trend by going to Google Trends and type in the main keyword for your product. Once there you will be able to see if your product is seasonal or not

Additionally, seasonal items are something you'll want to avoid. The rationale for this is that if I offer a Halloween-themed product, it will undoubtedly be profitable between October and November. That is all. In addition to that, there will be no sales until the following year. Therefore, avoid that. There are methods for determining whether a product is seasonal, and you may do it within helium 10. That will be discussed later. Additionally, you can use Google Trends to determine whether a product is seasonal.

At least for your first product, selling a seasonal product is a bad idea. Once you've sold a few things and gained experience with Amazon FBA, you should absolutely consider selling a seasonal product.

Finding products with Amazon's best sellers

So the initial way of finding products we'll cover is by searching through Amazons's best seller list. Go to "Amazon Best Sellers" (https://www.amazon.com/Best-Sellers). As you can see from the above images, these products are the best sellers on Amazon right now. Now you can not only look at Amazon's best sellers in the broad category but also search in the sub-categories.

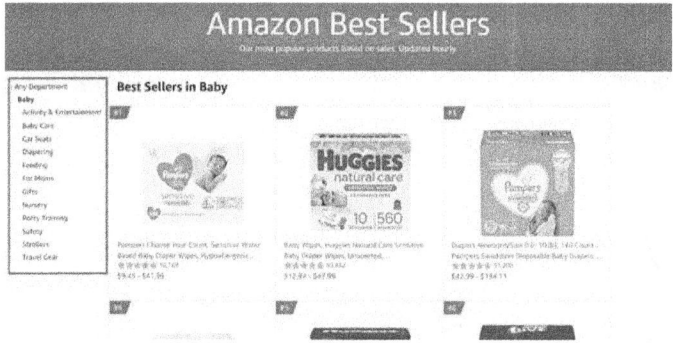

So the first picture shows you the best sellers in Amazon's baby section. Now the above image shows you the subcategories of baby products. Look at the left side of the image.

Search deeper and deeper. Check out all these subcategories.

Check out all the best-selling products, but also notice the section called "Frequently Brought Together." So, for instance, instead of selling one product in one category, you can create a package and sell it on Amazon. You can create several packages and offer your customers a discount if they buy the package. It is a win-win situation because customers are buying these items together anyway, and you offering them a discount makes them more motivated to buy from you. On the other hand, giving a discount means you earn a little less but buy and sell more products. So at the end of the day, you still make a hefty profit.

Once you have chosen a few products that you like, you need to collect all the information about that product. Product ratings will give you some valuable insight into the products. In particular, 1 and 2-star reviews will reveal a lot of information you need. They will tell you what this product is lacking, which aspects of this product customers didn't like, and so on.

So read all the negative 1 and 2-star reviews and think about how you can improve on them. This will help you stand out from the crowd and will help you tremendously to become a successful Amazon seller. Note the negative points from the customers and discuss with your supplier how they can provide you with better products that don't have these flaws.

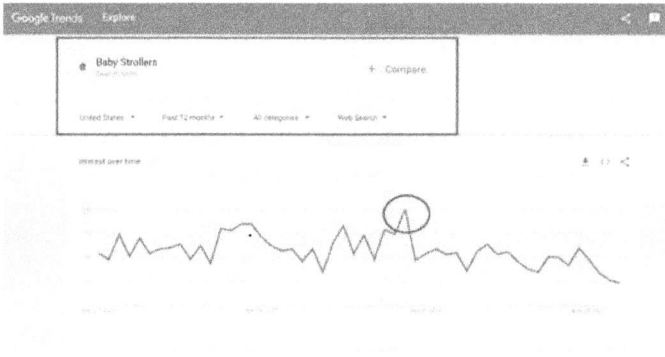

Remember, in business, timing is everything. You need to sell the right product at the right time. To understand things better, go to Google Trends and search for "baby strollers" using the marked search parameters. The above graph shows you That there are no seasonal trends so this s a good year round product to have.

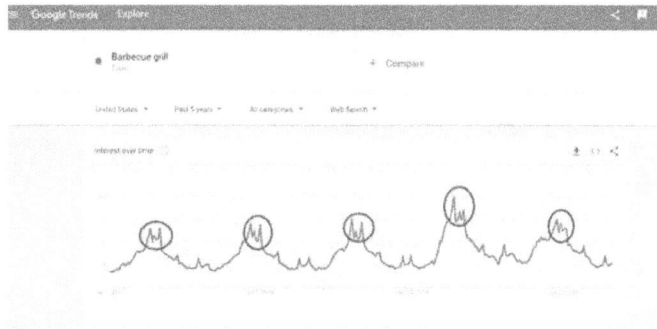

Here is another example with a barbecue grill. You can see it is a very seasonal item and sales go up and down at specific times of the year. With something like this you would want to order your product so that it arrives in spring so you can take advantage of the summer peak. Then when autumn hits you could limit your stock or avoid restocking at all until the next season.

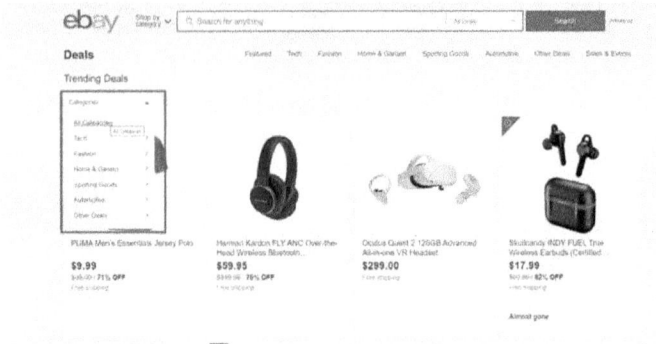

Now go to eBay and find out which products are the top-selling on eBay. Then see if those products are available on Amazon or not. If eBay's top-selling products are not sold on Amazon, then that is a terrific opportunity for you to start selling those products and establish your Amazon business.

Then you need to go to WatchCount.com, which is a site that lists eBay customer reviews of top-selling eBay products. From this site, you will get an idea of which products are in demand and not available on Amazon.

Then go to AliExpress and do the same.

Finding product with product research tools

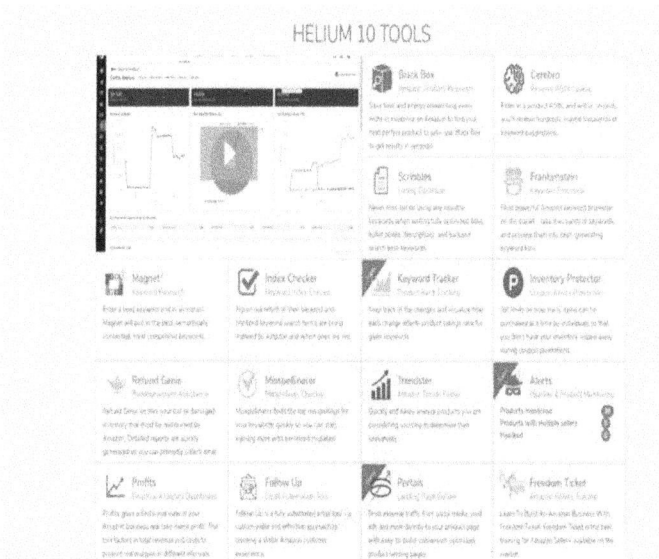

There are many product research tools out there that you can explore all with different pricing plans and features. They're designed to help you be able to search through Amazon's product catalog with little to no effort and should definitely be considered during the product research phase. You can learn more about different tools that you can purchase by searching online but for this book we'll be using Helium 10.

Helium 10 will be used to locate our merchandise, specifically the black box. What we're dealing with is rather straightforward. We're going to filter. We use particular criteria here to narrow our search and locate products that meet our criteria. Helium 10 will help us accomplish this. It retrieves and locates products for you based on the filters you provide.

Now, in terms of the categories, we're going to choose from, they're going to be some of my personal favorites. Tools and home improvement are good, pet supplies are good as well. Patio, lawn, and garden are decent, kitchen and dining are good. Industrial science is one of my favorites. Home and kitchen are good, households pretty decent. Stay away from handmade products and grocery products. You don't want to do those for the time being. Along with electronics, stay away from those three. Babbie products are very good, automotive is good. The thing about Babbie products is that it can be a little bit saturated. But obviously, baby products are pretty much always going to be in demand. Now, I'm going to choose tools and home improvement, pet supplies, and my favorite industrial and scientific.

Previously, we discussed the criteria that we're going to type in when looking for products. Now we'll add a minimum revenue of around 5000 dollars. The reason for this being that we want our product to earn us a decent amount for our investment every month and if we're making a 10-20% final profit margin having a product that does at least 5000 in revenue will net us a decent amount every month. The minimum price for the product, I want to set the price between 17 and 75 dollars. Anything less than that and it'll be hard to make a profit and above that you're getting out of that impulse buy zone. Now set the max amount of reviews to 75 that way you'll know if you can compete in that niche as a new seller.

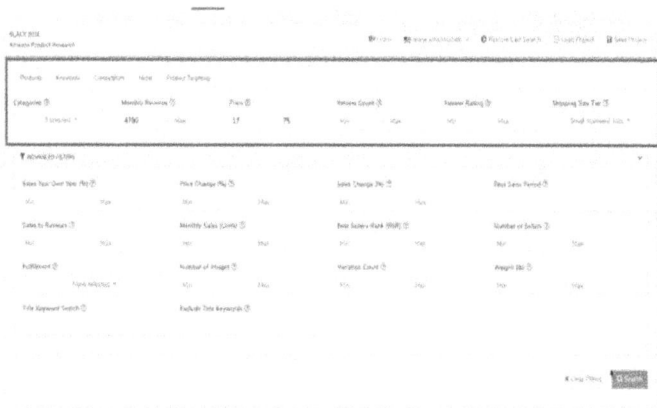

In terms of the shipping tier, let's start with a small standard size and large one. I know I mentioned that you should stay away from larger products, but in certain situations, it could make sense to have a product that's a little bit heavier or larger as long as the margins are there. So keep your options open. Now we're all set. I'm going to hit search and I'm going to go through all of my products here for me to develop.

You can see you'll get a result with many options for you. Things like a dog harness. if you're a dog owner, you're going to have a dog harness, for the most part. I look for unique products and it's going to seem pretty vague right now, but you'll definitely get an understanding as we decide to select some products here.

This is industrial and scientific.

This looks kind of interesting. Asbestos test kit. We're going to check this. Asbestos sample testing. What I look for when I look at a listing is to see if it has potential. I want to look at this and see if it sticks out right when I buy this product. The bullet points are pretty decent, they're pretty good. They have images there to help highlight the bullet points. The photos are photoshopped, but they're OK. You can certainly do better. It could use some professional photos to help it stick out. The description is pretty decent, It has instructions there, which is OK. Usually what I like to do is I like to have an HTML-based product description with additional bullet points in here, but this is OK too. It's an OK listing and I see why it is doing pretty well.

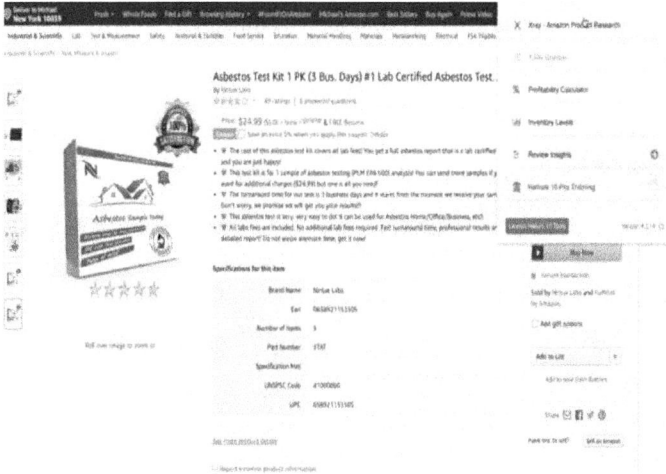

Now, what I want to do is take a look at Helium 10, the Chrome extension, and check for the revenue.

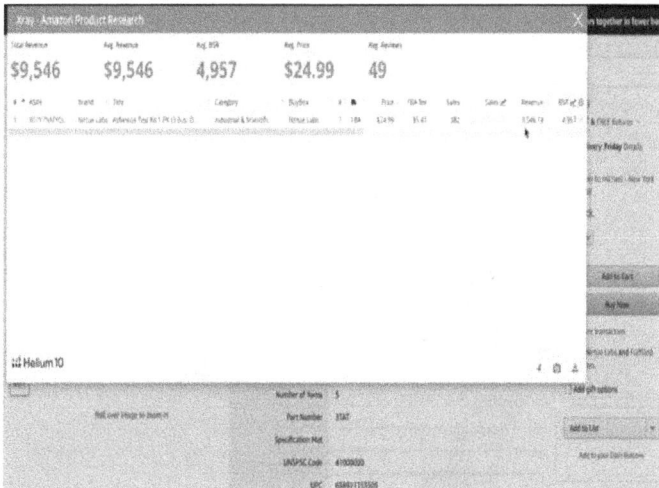

So it's doing about 9500. 382 sales a month. It's priced at $25, and that fee that Amazon takes away is 5.41 so that's not too bad. This looks pretty decent in terms of this listing and the potential, but now I want to check the competition, the level of competition.

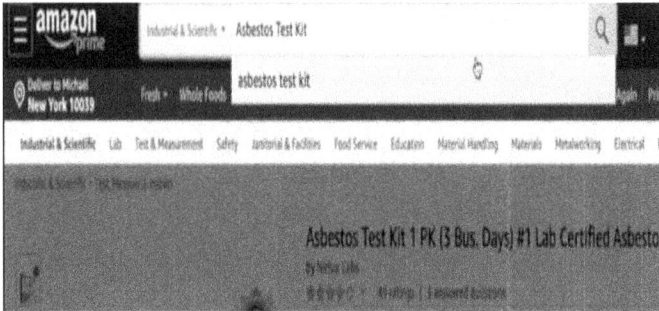

What I do is I just copy the main keyword that I think this would fall under and that's usually in the title. This is the main description for this product "asbestos test kit." I'm just going to plug that into the search and I look at the top.

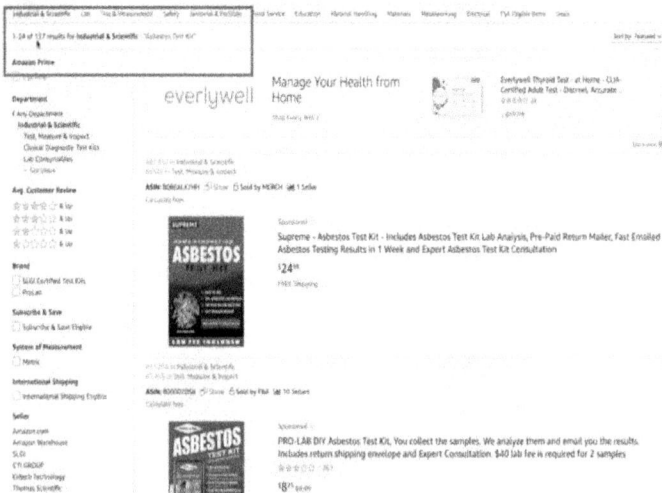

So you'll see there are 137 results, which is very low. Now that doesn't mean that every single one of these products, all 137 of them, is going to be an asbestos kit.

Now, the only thing with this product, if you were to select it, you want to be careful because there could be certain restrictions around selling something like this. So before even considering purchasing it, you'll have to do some research to see if Amazon would let you sell it. Let me just go back. Once I enter the main keyword, I want to stay in the search results, and then I want to hit the chrome extension.

The helium 10 chrome extension, because what it does is it's going to bring up every single product detail for every single product that shows up in this search result. So let's take a look.

Asbestos test kit 2500, and that sells for $8. What's the difference between this one and this one? Asbestos 15000 has 312 reviews. These are just different sizes. I would probably stay away from it. You don't want to go through the hassle of trying to get approved to sell an asbestos test kit on Amazon, so let's keep proceeding along. I'm looking for things that are pretty unique. I'm looking for unique products. I know that's pretty vague, but once you search and get used to this, you'll find a product that'll stand out.

Do 25 to 55. Review the count of 100 and see what this brings up. 168 products.

Well, this is interesting. A recovery sleeve for a dog. The only thing with these is that you have to have various products, different sizes, which could be a little bit of a pain, but again, sometimes it's worth it.

So when checking out the competion listing you want to see if they've got good pictures here, professional pictures with the dog actually using the product. Check out the bullet points and brand registry really get an idea of the product and if it's something that interests you in selling

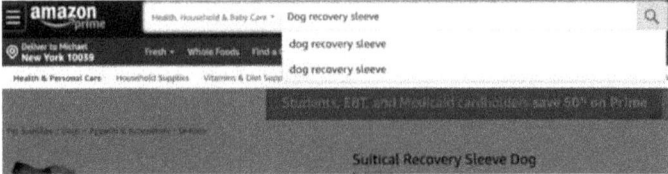

I'm going to see how the competition overall on Amazon is. We just type in "dog recovery sleeve."

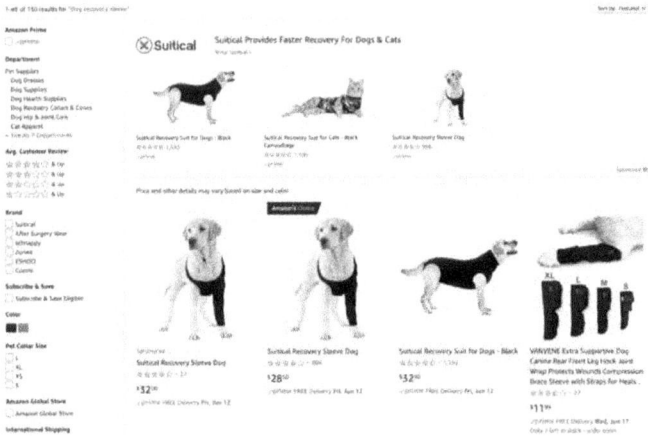

One hundred and thirty results. There's not that much competition. This could be a very good product. It's just one of those products where, you have to have all different sizes, just because dogs obviously come in all different shapes and sizes.

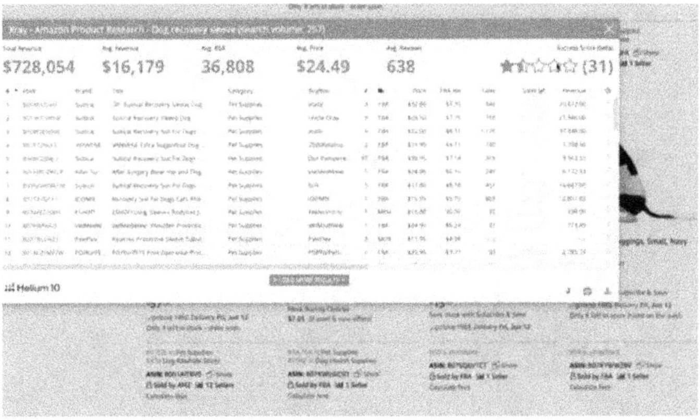

This category is a good fit. Also, by the way, don't pay attention to the "success score" on the above image because it is still in the beta stage.

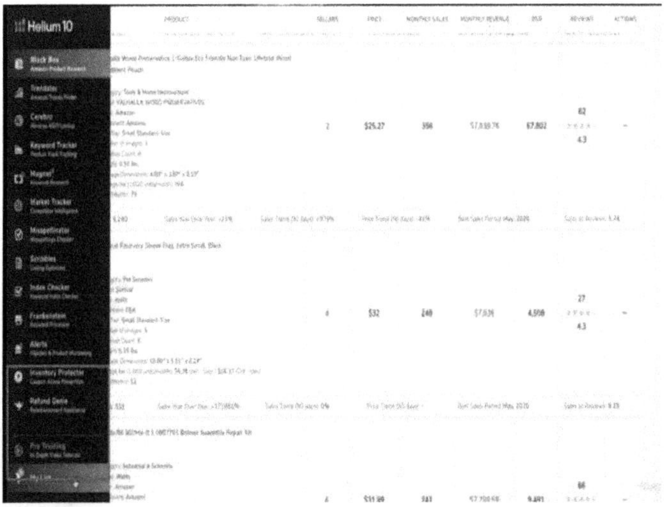

So you can add this to your list along with helium 10. Just by clicking here. And what that does is add it to your list, which can be found in the bottom left corner.

Recovery suit for dogs. This has a lot of ratings, too. But again, even though it has a lot of ratings,

the competition is very low overall. There are only three pages. So the success rate here is going to be very, very high just because there isn't much competition.

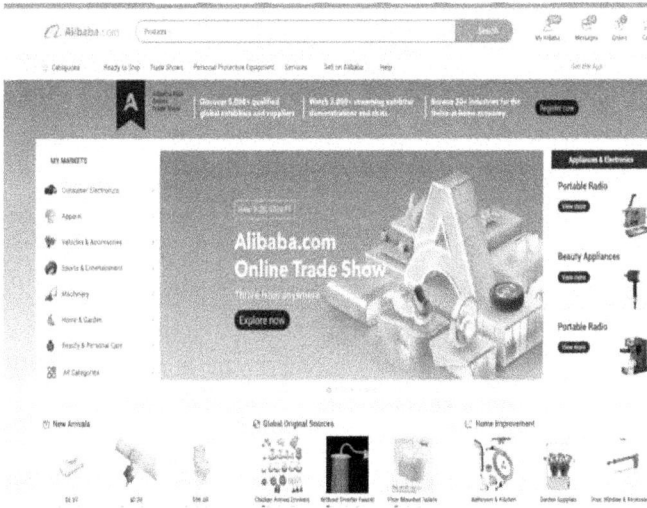

My next step would be to go to. Alibaba. Alibaba is basically, a website where you can search for manufacturers and suppliers across the world, mainly China.

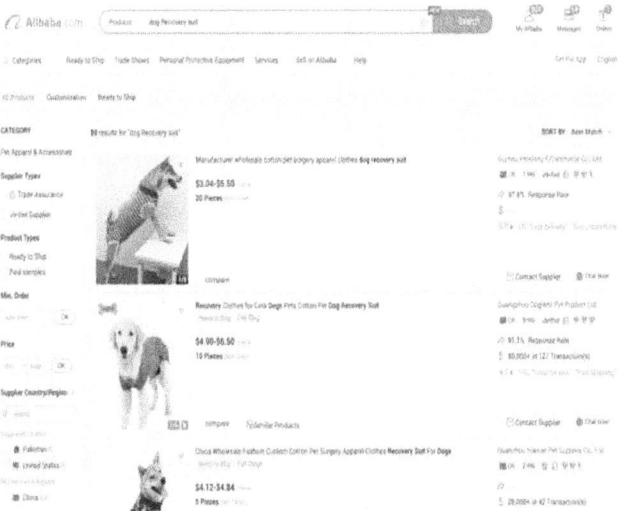

You're going to put in the same exact keyword that you used on Amazon. So dog recovery suit. Now we're going through Alibaba because we want to see how profitable this product can be for us. We're just going to get an estimate. It's an idea of what our returns could possibly be before we reach out to the supplier.

The reason why we're building this list of products is that we want to review those products, see which works best and narrow those down a little bit. And then we can go ahead and then reach out to the supplier. But now, we just want to see the potential profit for some of these products.

I always start with the higher number, the higher price here, just because to start, you're probably going to be ordering the minimum amount. In this case, the minimum order requirement is going to be 20 pieces, which isn't much. That's another good thing about this company. You could order a small amount. Just to test to see if this product works. Let's just say it costs $8 for this product, which is probably pretty light. Let's just say it cost $8 total, including shipping to get the product from China to the Amazon warehouse. OK, so eight dollars total per unit.

No, we will go back to Amazon and find the most similar.

This is probably the exact same one. It looks exactly the same, just with a different pattern. Here it is selling for $37. Well, it depends on the size. See, buying options. They're all 37, and let's just say it costs eight dollars to have this made and shipped to the Amazon warehouse.

Then you're looking at a net profit of eighteen dollars and 40 cents per unit sold. That's very high. That's very good. Now, obviously, there's going to be the cost of advertising included with this as well, which isn't included with this. So you'll see this pop up when you install the Helium 10 Chrome Extension.

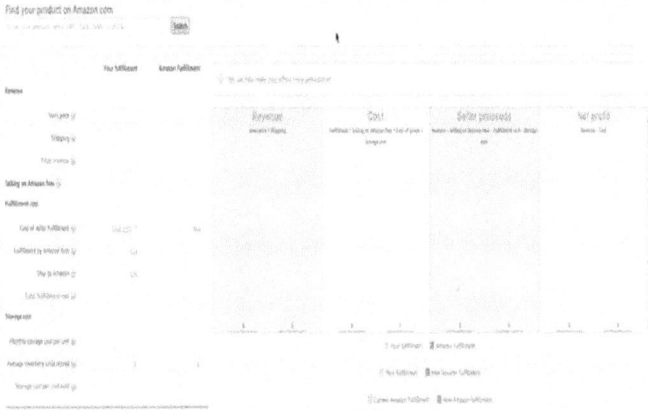

One other thing I'd like to do is search for an FBA Calculator. Amazon has its own calculator as well. This is pretty much the same thing as this, but I like to get the actual profit margin number. And I'll show you why.

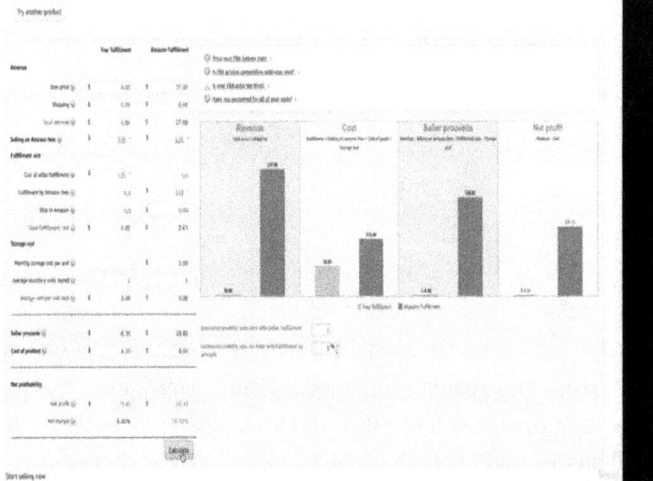

It brings up that product, and again, the cost of the product total, including shipping, was $8.50. The product is selling at $37, so those returns are really good. It's twenty dollars and thirty-two cents.

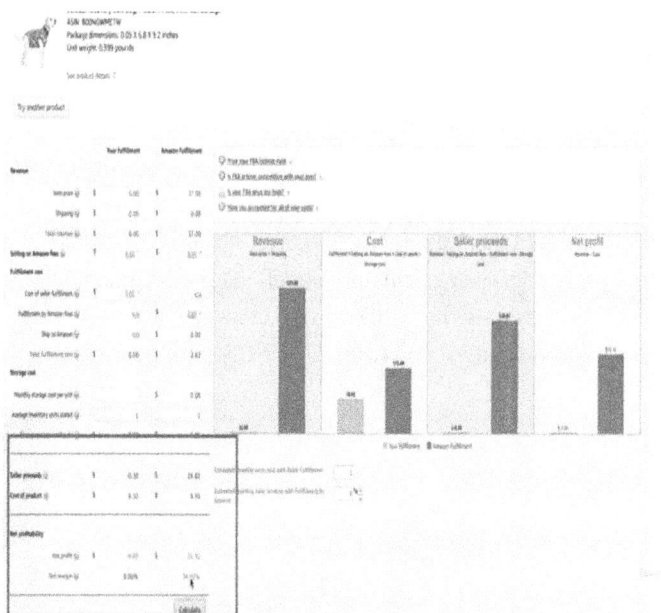

Look at that fifty-five percent profit margin. That's amazing. You can start selling this product right now. It would be very easy to get this up and running on Amazon. And, you know, you can make a lot of money doing this, and it's lightweight, so this is the ideal product.

And again, let me just make it clear that the net margin is a very important number, especially when you are doing advertising. Once you go over this percentage, you will start losing money on your advertising. When you're doing ads, you'll see something called "ACOS". And when you're running your ads, it's going to show you your costs. And if you exceed this number, that means you lose money on every single sale. But if you're below that number, then that means you're still profitable.

Determining If A Product Is Seasonal

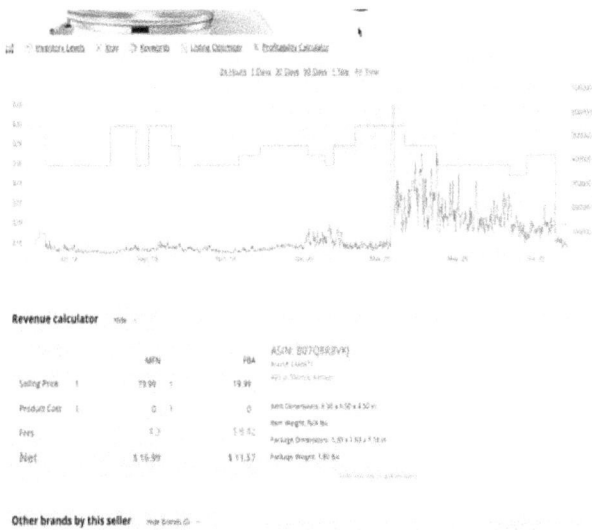

Now I want to go into more detail about checking a product for seasonality and making sure that it's going to consistently sell throughout the course of a full year. I talked about it before in slight detail, but now we are going to discuss it in detail. That way, you'll have the full resources to check for seasonality. We are going to use helium 10. It has a chrome add-on that allows you to check for seasonality within the graph. Basically, if you go to a listing that you are looking into and you take a look at the chart, I'm going to show you how to read this chart and check for seasonality.

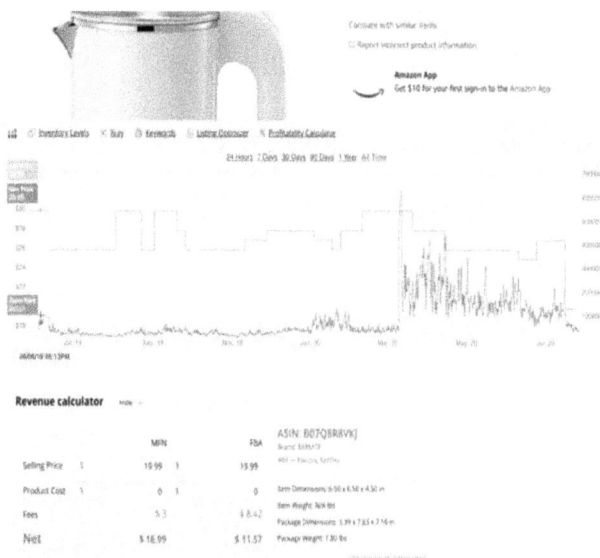

This is a very good example because of what's been going on with the pandemic. We have a good understanding of what trends look like. This product looks like it started probably at the beginning of June 2019, and as you can see here, it is tracking the sales rate through July of 2000. So up until now, and it looks pretty consistent, the sales rank is pretty stable. It is performing really well.

And then, all of a sudden, you're going to see, in March of that year, this spike. Why? The reason is that's when the coronavirus hit the country. So people stopped traveling.

And as you can see, this is a portable travel electric kettle suitable for traveling, cooking, and boiling. So it makes sense that people began to travel less, naturally at the time and still today.

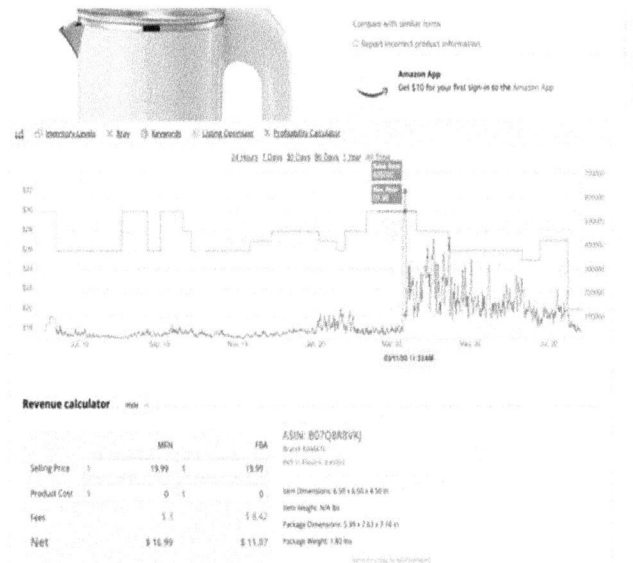

So sales declined, and you could see that the spike was the reason. There are a lot of peaks and a lot of valleys. It's just really inconsistent. The overall trend is headed downward. This is a good example. That's how you're going to check for seasonality for products.

If you look at the Halloween products, you are going to see the exact same thing.

There will be a lot of fluctuation and then, all of a sudden, a big spike around Halloween. During the fall, it is going to start to decline and then go back up. So you probably want to stay away from something like this.

That's how you check for seasonality within a listing using the helium 10 and its chrome extension, and then, you're going to use Google Trends as well. So, similarly to what we just saw on the product listing, we're going to check Google Trends and look for any fluctuations here. This is over the past year's Google searches for portable kettles. You can check overall and see if it continues that trend. But it's probably safe to say that it's going to still go up and down pretty much and fluctuate over the next couple of months. So that's how you check thoroughly for seasonality and to see if a product is going to sell well throughout the course of the year.

There's one more thing I wanted to show you here within the helium 10 tool. If you go to your list of saved products, it's going to check the sales year over year.

Obviously, it has to be around for longer than a year to extrapolate that data. You can use this as well to check for trends as well as look at the listings within the Helium 10 extension.

How To Check If A Product Is Patented

Something you should be doing before you go ahead and order the product from the manufacturer (even when you're in the product research phase) is to check if the product is patented already. That's going to be very important. You don't want to get to that point where you have a product or the inventory ordered and then go ahead and have it listed on Amazon only for it to be removed. So this is a pretty important step in the process.

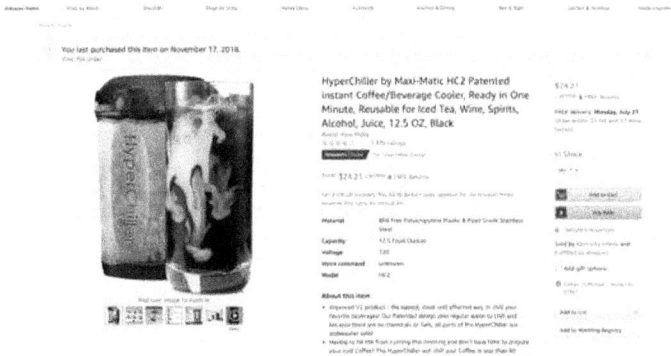

Always check to see if there's a patent on the product before you go ahead and order inventory. This is why you always want to have a list of 10 to 15 products. So you can sell other products if one of your products gets removed by Amazon. So here's how you check. This is actually a pretty cool product. Check it out. It's called the "hyper chiller." You can check if a product is patient with a few simple steps. You can either go to the "USPTO" website or you can go to Google Patents, which I find to be a lot easier.

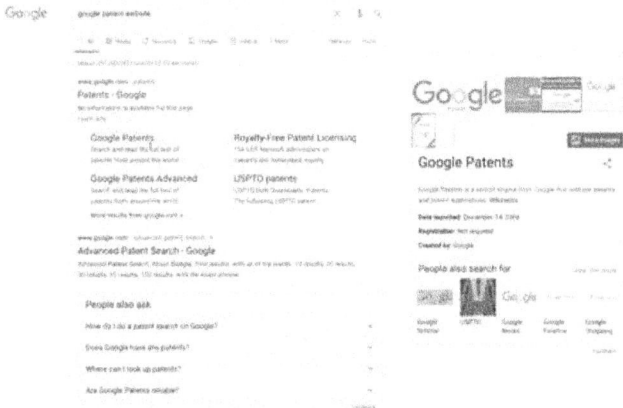

Type in "Google patents" and you'll see it right here. What I typically do is I'll put in the brand name first to see if anything comes up, and I'll just take the brand name HyperChiller. See what the searchers say. Look, it's pretty straightforward: beverage and product cooler.

The utility relates to the kitchen and equipment. Drinks are made at the food cooler. in the form of a container. Yep, this product is patented and you can't sell it. Descriptions of these products aren't always accurate, but this product is patent.

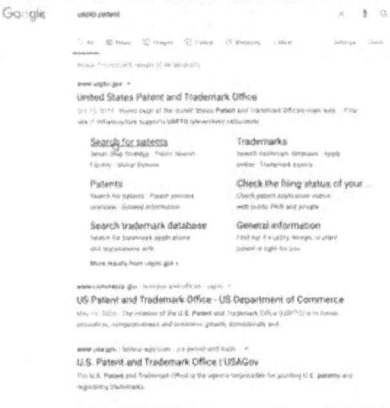

You can also check the USPTO site for patents. Go to Google, and type in "uspto patent" and search for patterns.

And then a quick search, and if I were to type in "hyper chiller" here, yes, it's the same thing.

It was first filed on October 12, 2017. Usually there's an expiration date on here somewhere. It's pretty straightforward. I can't sell this one.

Sometimes a product's name mentions that it is patented, like this.

One other thing you can do is to check if there is a pattern or not when you do a Google search for the product on Amazon. If you're literally the only person selling it, or if there's only one other person selling that product, there could be a good chance that there's a patent on that product. So you always want to check in on that scenario as well, because usually the best-selling products have at least two or three other people selling them. But that's how you go ahead and do a patent.

How to Confirm That Your Product Is Eligible To Sell On Amazon

.

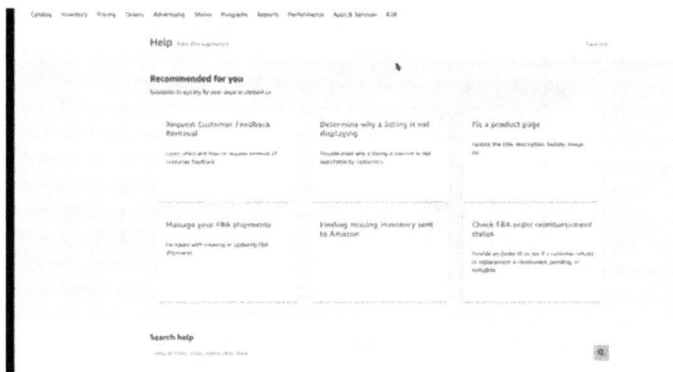

Let's talk about restricted products. A restricted product is something that you need to get approval for from Amazon before you can sell that product. You want to do this before you go ahead and order inventory from your supplier. You don't want the product to arrive at Amazon and then find out that you know you aren't able to sell this product. There are a few ways to check if a product is restricted. Before you buy the product, go into the Amazon Seller Central and reach out to Amazon seller support.

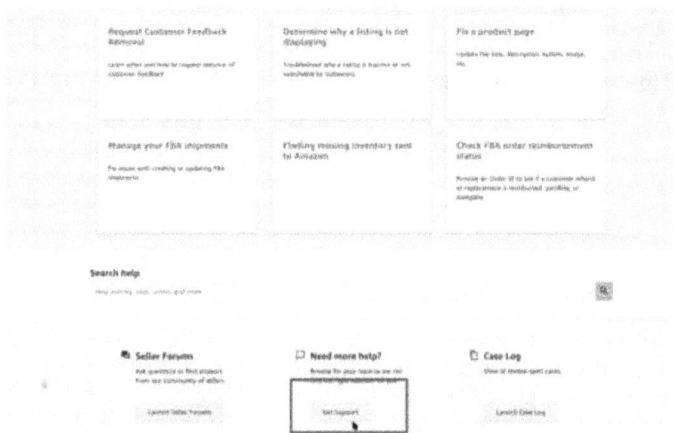

It's basically customer service for sellers. You can do this by clicking the top right help section, and then towards the bottom of the screen, you're going to see get support. Need more help?

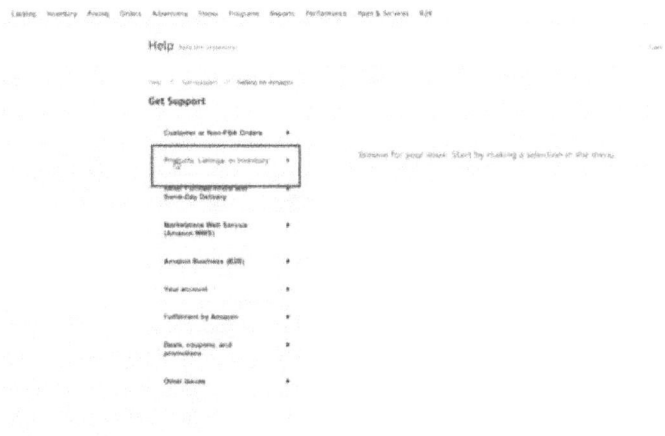

Get support. Selling on Amazon and then clicking the products, listings, or inventory dropdown, and then you're going to see a couple of things here.

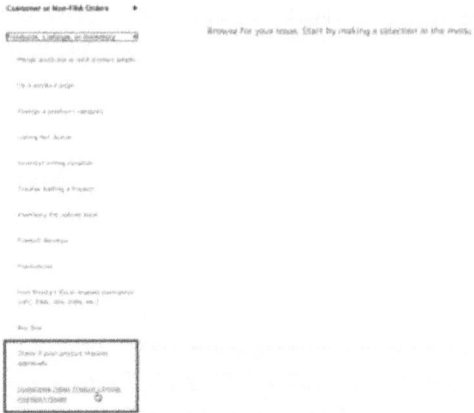

We're going to focus on the bottom two and investigate other products, listings, and inventory issues, as well as check if your product requires approval. So let's do this first.

Check if your product requires approval.

Get Support

And this is going to give you a list of restricted products. So we're going to be able to see everything in detail. Certain categories require you to obtain a pre-approval from Amazon before listing in those categories.

Restricted products

Restricted products

- Recalled
- Animals & Animal Related Products
- Art - Fine Art
- Art - Home Decor
- Automotive and Powersports
- Composite Wood Products
- Cosmetics & Skin/Hair Care
- COVID-19 Supplies
- Currency, Coins, Cash Equivalents, and Gift Cards
- Dietary Supplements
- Drugs & Drug paraphernalia
- Electronics
- Explosives, Weapons, and Related Items
- Export Controls
- Food & Beverage
- Gambling & Lottery
- Hazardous and Dangerous Items
- Human Parts & Burial Artifacts
- Jewelry & Precious Gems
- Laser products
- Lighting
- Lock Picking & Theft Devices
- Medical devices and accessories
- Offensive and Controversial Materials
- Pesticides and Pesticide Devices
- Plant and Seed Products
- Postage Meters & Stamps
- Recalled Products
- Recycling electronics
- Subscriptions and Periodicals
- Surveillance Equipment

Among those restricted are alcohol, automotive, COVID-19 supplies, electronics, food and beverage, surveillance, and other products. Now you have a good idea of what that looks like. Refer to this, but also reach out to Amazon directly because sometimes this list changes. For instance, COVID 19, this obviously wasn't an issue 2 years ago, but now it is. Always reach out to customer support before you go ahead and purchase your products. Now we're going to go back and get support on Amazon product listings for inventory.

Click "Investigate other product listings". Inventory issues. So here we're just going to type it out.

We're messaging Amazon: Hi, I'm going to be selling a product similar to ASIN ……

So just in case you forget, ASIN is Amazon's dedicated number for classifying a product. It's essential for this product's name. Anytime you call seller support, you always bring up the ASIN that you are talking about.

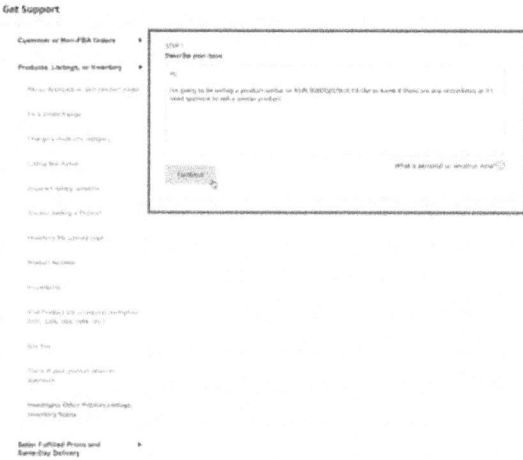

"I'm going to be selling a product similar to ASIN….. I'd like to know if there are any restrictions or if I need approval to sell a similar product." Click and send that information to them, and then you'll be all set.

You can give Amazon a phone call if you download their app and then click "seller support." They'll actually give you a call and you can speak to a support agent.Go ahead and get this done before you let the supplier know that you're going to be making a purchase, and you will be all set.

Profitability Check Learn Your Margins

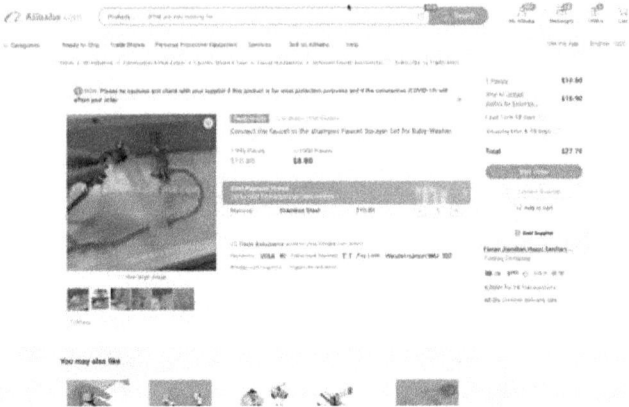

Now we need to do a profitability check. I know that we did this a little bit in an earlier segment, but I wanted to go ahead and do this again. This way, you will have a clear understanding of this concept. What we're looking at here is Alibaba. Before you go ahead and add a product to your list and before you reach out to a supplier, you want to make sure that you can make money off of this product. The way to do that is just to make an estimate on whether this product will be profitable for you, and you can do this by going to Alibaba.

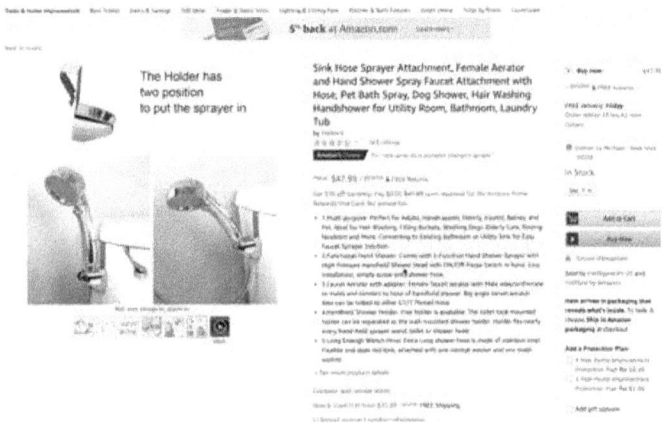

So let's say this is a product that I selected and I want to ensure that it is going to make money for me. This is very, very straightforward and simple to do.

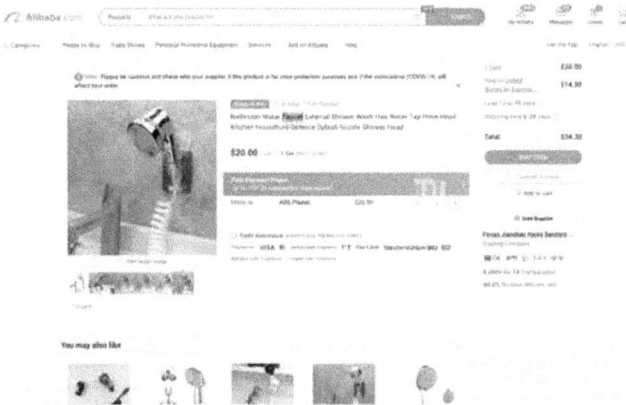

Go to Alibaba.

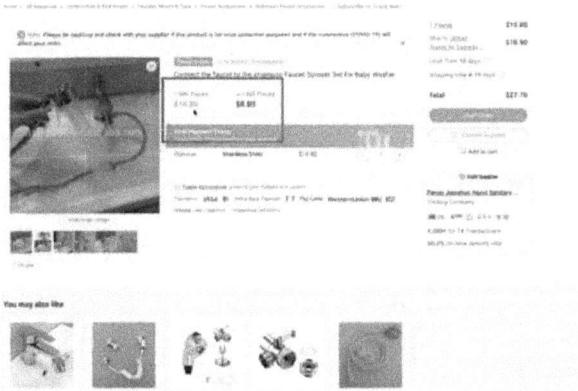

This might be the hardest part, (finding a similar product), but it took me about five minutes to find this product. Let's see how much it's selling for. On Alibaba, they are selling in bulk at $10.80 per unit. Then add an additional $2.50 for shipping. Let's just round up and make it $13 per unit if we were to go ahead with this product.

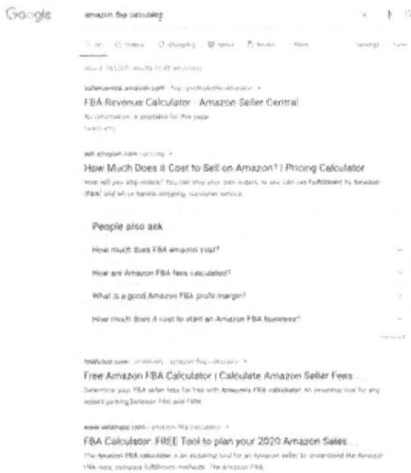

I typed into the Amazon FBA calculator $13.

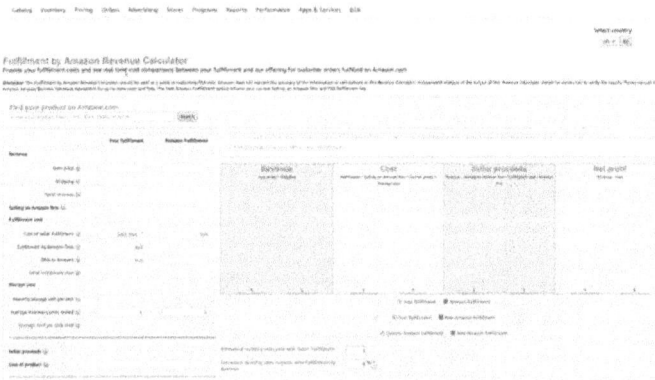

You can either go here and do this, or you can go directly to the listing and enter in the information. I like to do it here just because it gives you a better understanding, but you will need this ASIN here.

We'll utilize the Amazon FBA calculator's ASIN search because it's more accurate.

When you're using Helium 10, it does the same thing on the listing, but it doesn't give you the actual net margin. So we need $13 to buy the product in bulk, and it's selling for $47.99.

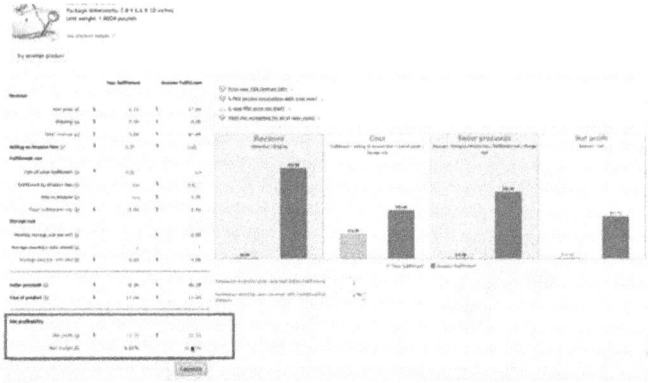

That comes out to be 46%. The profit margin is 46%, and the net profit is $22 per unit if you were to sell it at $47.99.

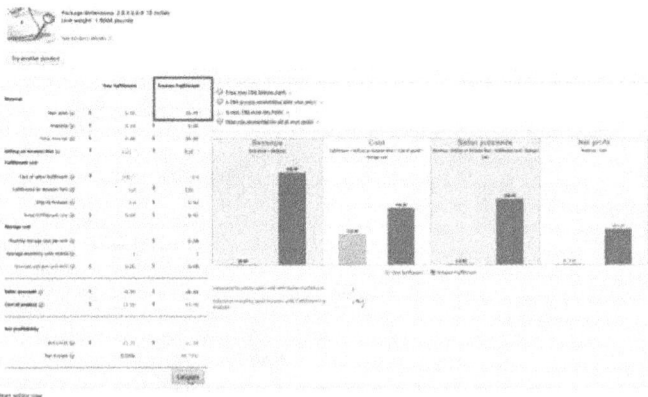

When you first start out as a new seller on Amazon, keep the prices low to sell more. When you first launch a product, you are not going to sell too many of them. Keep the prices low to sell more, such as around $40.

So let's say you are selling at $39.99. You are still making a profit of $15 a unit, which is fantastic. This is how you are going to do a profitability check. This percentage comes into play later with advertising.

Chapter Four

Finding the Manufacturer to Produce your Product

To become an Amazon seller, you may have to put in a lot of hard work. In order to get into a market, the first step is to find a product that fits your budget while still being within your reach. Creating a concrete product is the next step! As a first-time Amazon seller, you may be unsure how to locate manufacturers. Rest assured, though, that finding manufacturers is much simpler than you may imagine. Seasoned and first-time sellers alike may find it difficult to locate and source products from a manufacturer. This means you're looking for a supplier who will not only supply you with products but also help your company grow. Finding an experienced, trustworthy manufacturer who can consistently deliver high-quality products and offer value to the partnership is essential.

In this chapter, you'll learn how to choose and work with reputable manufacturers who can help you realize your brand's and private label's goals. When you find the proper manufacturer to partner with, you are essentially establishing the foundation for future brand-building opportunities. If the first product is successful and you are satisfied with the final product, you are likely to use the same supplier for future private-label products.

As a result, it's vital that you do your homework and thoroughly investigate any possible manufacturers before placing a bulk purchase and signing a contract in order to reduce the possibility of any complications.

Incoterms (International Delivery Terms)

The incoterms define the role between seller and buyer at an international transaction

- EXW
- FOB
- DDU
- DDP

Now we are going to discuss what "Incoterms" is. The word means "international delivery terms." You can say that they are transport terms. You need to understand these terms if you are making international exports or imports. With these terms, you are also making deals with your manufacturer. With these terms, you ask your manufacturer to ship your product to the U.S. You can't get started with Amazon FBA unless you understand these terms. These terms are extremely crucial because your suppliers will give you product prices based on these terms. Your aim is to get the product from your manufacturer and ship it to Amazon warehouses. You need the assistance of service providers known as freight forwarders to accomplish this. In the above image, you see four terms, but actually, there are twelve terms, but only these four are important for running an Amazon FBA as they transfer control of the product at the most convenient times during the shipping process. To ship products from China, we use these four terms. They are EXW, FOB, DDU, and DDP. These are the connections between your supplier and you. These terms indicate who will deal with taxes and who with customs procedures.

Export Packaging	Loading Charges	Delivery to Port/Place	Export Duty, Taxes & Customs Clearance	Origin Terminal Handling Charges	Loading on Carriage	Freight Charges	Insurance	Destination Terminal Handling Charges	Delivery to Destination	Unloading at Destination	Import Duty, Taxes & Customs Clearance
SELLER	BUYER	BUYER	BUYER	BUYER	BUYER	BUYER	Negotiable	BUYER	BUYER	BUYER	BUYER

EX Work (EXW)

In the case of the EXWorks Incoterm, the buyer takes full responsibility over the cargo as soon as it leaves the manufactures warehouse. Once the cargo has been picked up, the buyer is solely responsible for getting it to its final destination. Incoterm ExWorks is applicable to all modes of transportation, no matter how many legs are involved in the delivery. Once the cargo is loaded into export containers and picked up, the buyer has full responsibility over the shipment. This means that the buyer is responsible for all transportation and export documentation, as well as all freight costs. The buyer assumes responsibility for the products once they are removed from the seller's property. In order to avoid mistakes and unexpected charges associated with shipping and transporting the items, beginners and customers unfamiliar with exporting are advised to hire a freight forwarder.

Export Packaging	Loading Charges	Delivery to Port/Place	Export Duty, Taxes & Customs Clearance	Origin Terminal Handling Charges	Loading on Carriage	Freight Charges	Insurance	Destination Terminal Handling Charges	Delivery to Destination	Unloading at Destination	Import Duty, Taxes & Customs Clearance
SELLER	SELLER	SELLER	SELLER	SELLER	SELLER	BUYER	Negotiable	BUYER	BUYER	BUYER	BUYER

FOB (Free on Board)

FOB is when the manufacturer will handle getting the product from their ware house to an American port. Once the product is dropped off at a port, the buyer will either pick it up themselves or arrange with a freight forwarder to send it to them. It's the seller's responsibility to clear exports, and the buyer's responsibility to take care of products after they leave the port of entry. When requesting FOB prices, be sure to include the name of the port where the items will be delivered. Many people use this phrase to refer to an intercom system since an inspection service may easily access the export port to check the items for quality assurance. In addition, the seller is in charge of everything that happens in the country of origin. The buyer is in charge of everything once the items leave the country, which simplifies matters. Because most freight forwarders have offices near the port, they may easily pick up your products on your behalf and transport them to a third party landing facility (3PL) or directly into Amazon's warehouse. FOB is probably going to be the cheapest form of transporting cargo as many manufacturers are used to sending product to the Chinese port and then your freight forwarder can handle the rest once it's in America. However this form of transport can be a little tricker than EXW as coordinating the information between manufacturer and freight forwarder will be on a much more time-sensitive schedule.

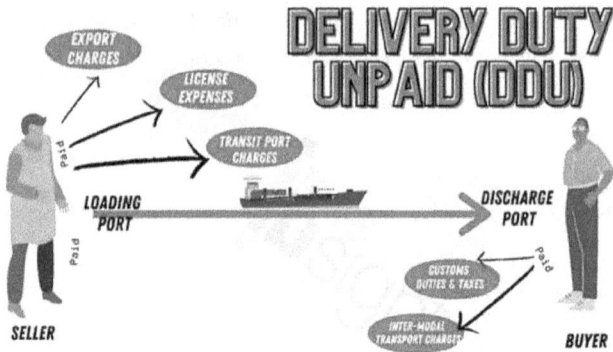

DDU (Delivered Duty Unpaid)

When items are sold "Delivered Duty Unpaid," the seller assumes all responsibility for their safe delivery to a specified location, pays for all transportation costs, and assumes all risks associated with shipping. Once the products have been delivered to the agreed-upon destination, the customer is responsible for paying import duties and any additional transportation fees. When a product is marked as "Delivered Duty Paid" (DDP), the seller is responsible for paying all import tariffs, customs clearing fees, and taxes.

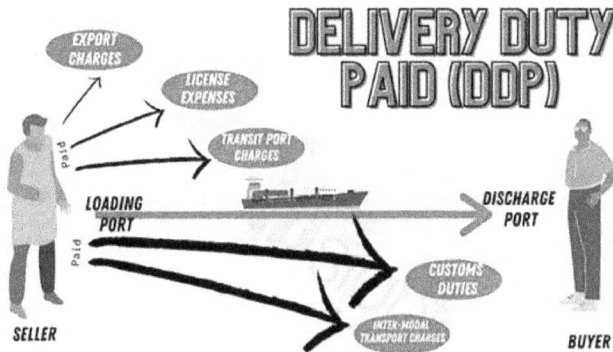

DDP (delivery duty paid)

Delivery duty paid (DDP) shipping is a kind of shipping in which the seller assumes responsibility for all shipping costs and risks until the items arrive at the buyer's desired location. The International Chamber of Commerce established DDP, a standardized shipping method used mostly for international shipping, to assist with standardizing shipping alternatives worldwide. DDP is a common shipping method only for air and maritime freight. DDP offers significant benefits to buyers by reducing their exposure to risk, responsibility, and expense. Because it may swiftly diminish revenues if handled incorrectly, DDP, while beneficial to buyers, maybe a significant headache for sellers. Given the complexity of international shipping rules and regulations, as well as the fact that each country has its own set of rules and laws controlling customs formalities, DDP is great for those new to Amazon FBA and who don't want a lot of stress but will usually end up costing the most to you as the buyer, because of this I only recommend it for first time buyer's. generally to maximize profits shipping with EXW or FOB is a better option and isn't that much harder so if you don't mind taking the extra step of hiring a freight forwarder I would avoid shipping using DDU or DDP altogether.

Find Suppliers

Now we are going to discuss how to find the best manufacturers in the entire world. The relationship that you have with your manufacturer will be one that is either very good or very bad and can make or break your business so we're going to cover how to find the best manufacturers for you now. First, go to Alibaba.com. Most of the things that you're probably wearing on your body were made by manufacturers that are listed on this site.

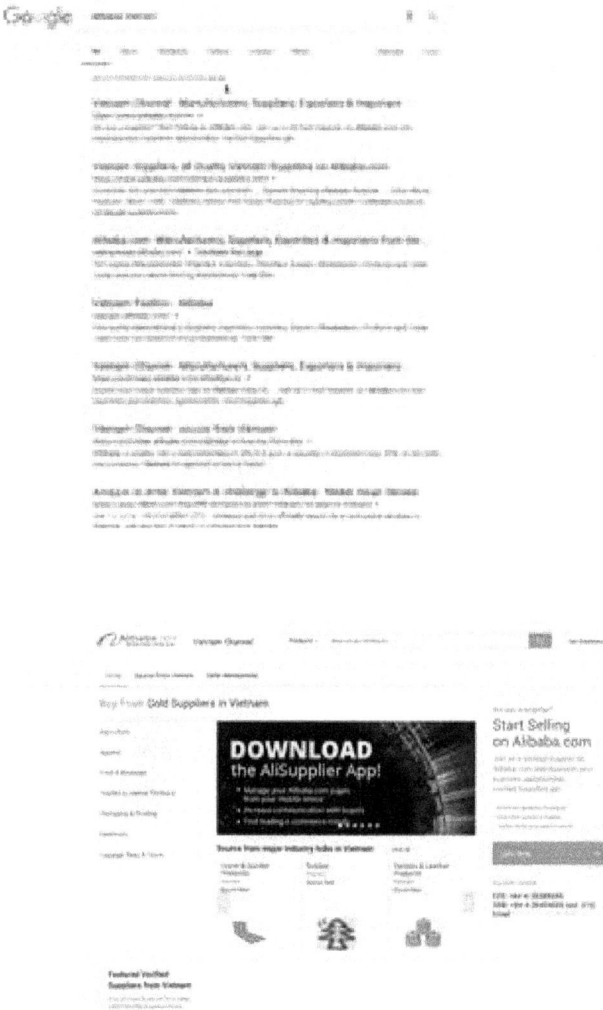

This is basically like a massive directory of manufacturers, most of which are based in China, but there's also Alibaba Vietnam and Alibaba India. On Alibaba, you need to find a reliable manufacturer because you do not want to work with a wholesaler or a middleman. You want to find the person that's going to give you the absolute lowest possible price so you can make a good profit. The lowest possible price means more profit. So let's dive in on exactly how we're going to find the best manufacturers.

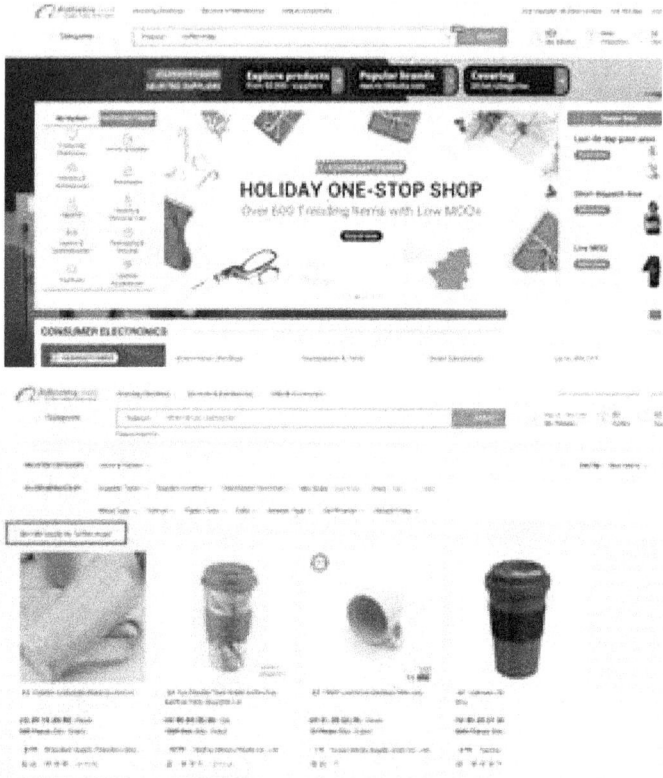

For example, if I want to find someone to make coffee mugs, I just searched and there are literally 2501102 results for coffee mugs, which is too high. So, instead of doing it by-products (because most of these listings are individual listings and many of them are actually created by the same supplier). If you send emails to different product manufacturers, they might be the same manufacturer.

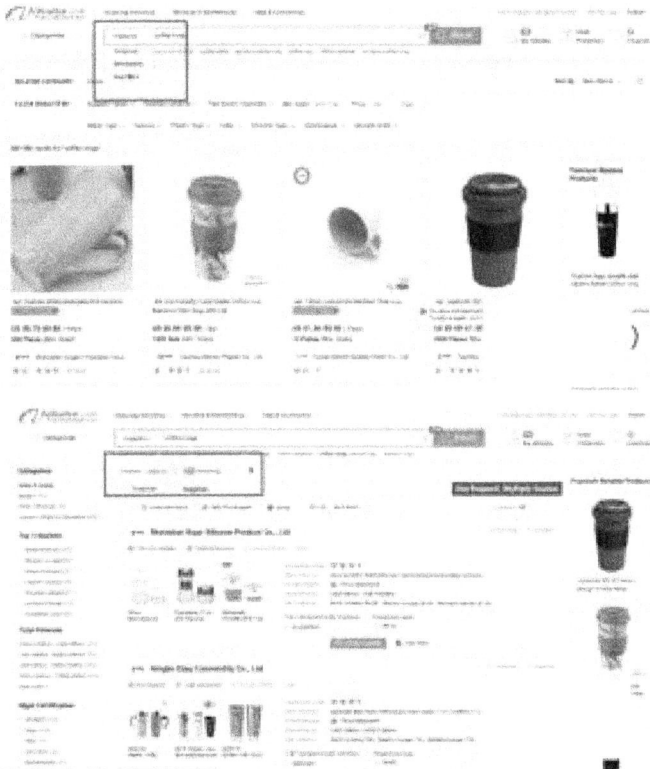

Do not use "products" when searching. Use the word "supplier" when searching. So now there are fewer than 2000 results, which makes your job easier and saves time. With this method, you don't have to send emails to 25,000 people.

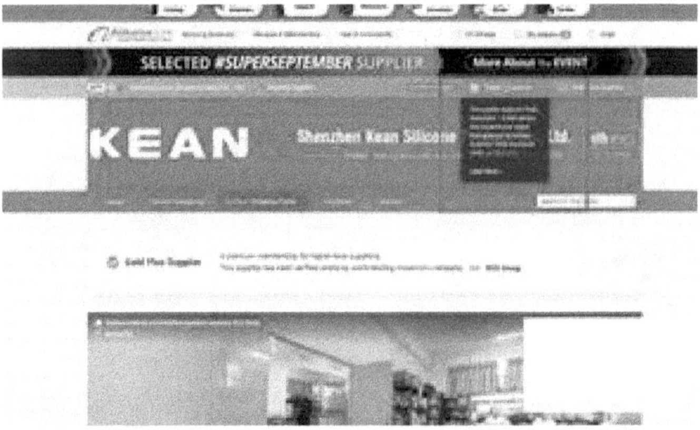
SELECTED #SUPERSEPTEMBER SUPPLIER
KEAN

SELECTED #SUPERSEPTEMBER SUPPLIER
KEAN

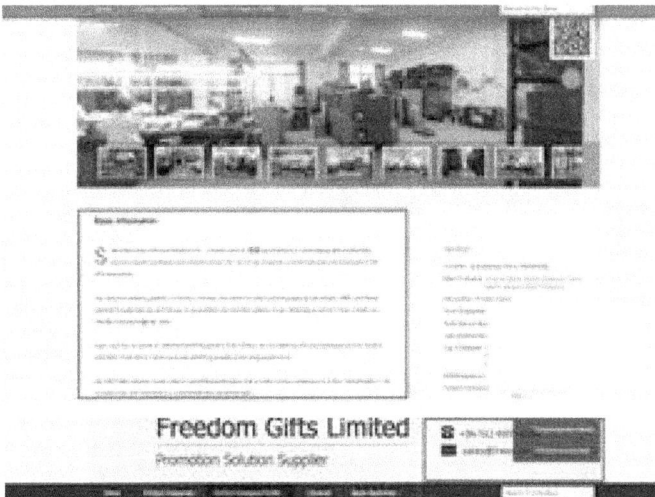

Let's choose one, for example, "Shenzhen Kean silicone." They have a verified company profile, and you can see some pictures of their factory here. They have a few pictures of their operational factory and use state-of-the-art materials. Here is some information about the company: The company started in 2006. At this company, 100 to 200 people work. This company is an established one. It seems that you can trust them. They also have ISO certification, which is good. I am now going to read a few reviews.

There are only 14 reviews, but they will reveal some important information to you. After doing some research on this company, I feel good that I can do business with them. They have email addresses and phone numbers, so you can contact them. You can see that they are "Gold Plus Suppliers." This means that they are serious about selling products on Alibaba. So you can trust this supplier. You know they will supply you with your products on time. You can use PayPal to pay your manufacturer and use Skype or Zoom to communicate.

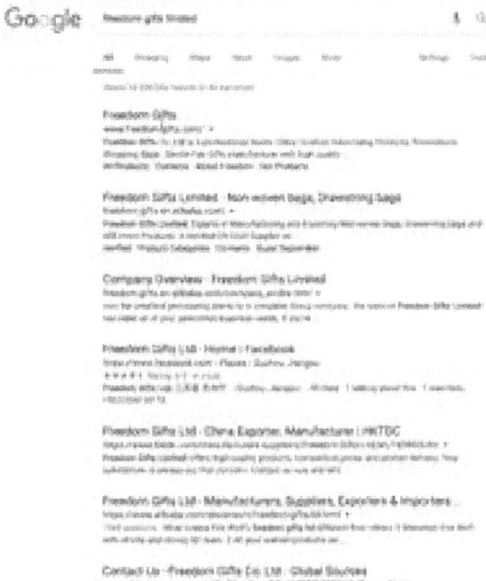

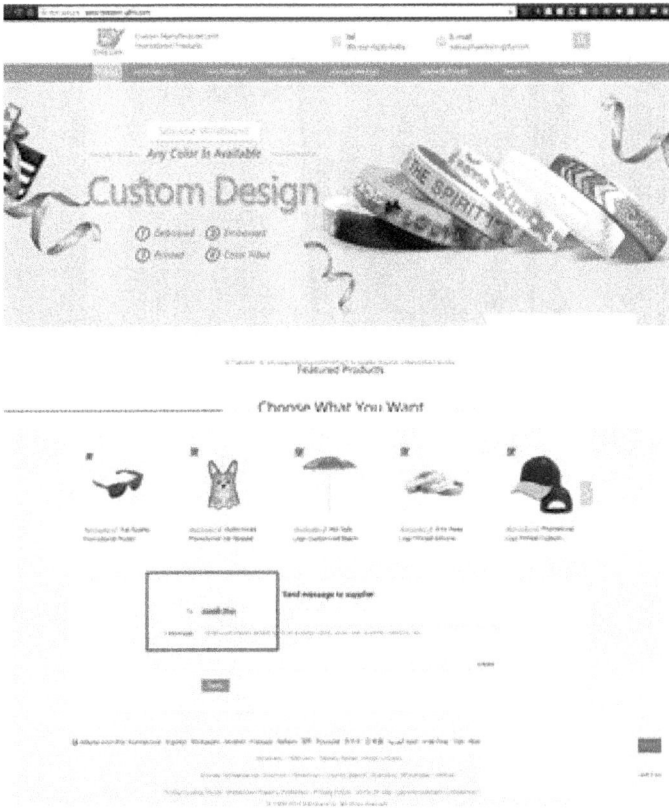

I am going to research another company now. Freedom Gifts Limited, I believe, is a massive company. I have done business with them. They are a reputable company with a premium membership. They got Alibaba certification, like gold supplier and trade assurance. They have a nice website. When you're ready to reach out to a supplier or suppliers you need to log into your account and enter your inquiry details, such as product name, color, size, etc.

Also, it is important that you give the product description accurately. The best way to get it is by sending a link of a similar product on amazon directly to the manufacturer. For example, use this link to visit the Amazon product page and just copy-paste the part and include it in your email to the supplier. Once you give the manufacturer all your product specifications you'll want to order a sample of the product to ensure it's of a high quality. While you always are trying to lower costs it is not always best to go with the cheapest manufacturer if the quality of the end product is going to be substantially lower. Remember to buid a successful brand on amazon you need something that will please the end user and that means you aren't going to be able to buy low quality goods that break or have a lot of defects if you want to achieve long term viability.

Inventory forecasting

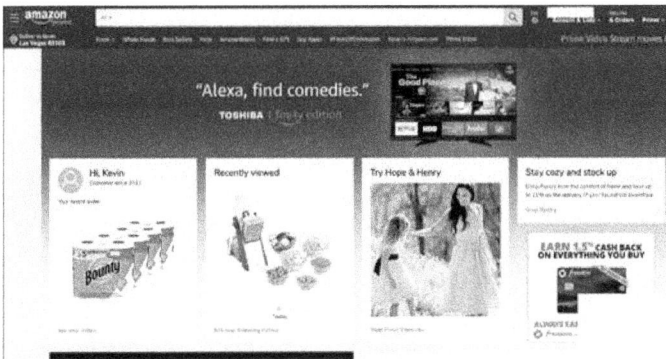

Now we are going to discuss how many units you should order on your first order. There are a couple of ways to do this. Most people know it as inventory forecasting. First we are going to discuss the easier method. Then the harder, but more accurate method. You use a simple spreadsheet with this I-99 cart trick method. With this method, you add products that you're interested in getting into that niche to your cart. Maybe you add five of the top products on Amazon's first page, like the top five organic listings, to your cart. Now if you change the number of units in your cart to 999 if the seller on amazon has less than that you will receive an error and then you'll see the exact amount of units that the seller has in stock at amazon's warehouse. On the first day, you notice that maybe there are 500 left.

And then the next day, there were 490, then 480. You can tell that it is selling 10 units per day. And what you really want is to track five, or even ten, different products on page one for three days. And then you want to get an average of how many products and how many units are selling per day.

That is the hard but accurate way. Doing the I-99 kart track method means just having a simple spreadsheet with the product that you decide that you want to sell. Calculating the overall average, maybe this product sells 10 today. The second product sells 20 a day, and the third product sells 15 a day. So then, the overall average would be 15 units per day. Once you have that number, the average number of products sold per day, it facilitates inventory forecasting. It is extremely simple to predict how many units you'll sell a day and from that number you can determine how many you'll need to order to have a 3 month supply of product. Now, we're going to talk about a couple of things, and then we're going to talk about how to actually do this.

The reason why we do things the way we do them is more or less because of inventory storage fees and long-term storage fees. I recommend you read these sections.

You can see that long-term storage fees are 6.9 dollars per cubic foot.

Normal storage fees are $.90 per cubic foot. That is a massive difference. It is 10 times more expensive, so you need to be careful about it. How do you actually incur long-term storage fees?

You can incur long-term storage fees for inventory that has been in the Amazon US fulfillment centers for more than 365 days. You never want to have any products in an Amazon warehouse for more than a year. What this means is that if you order a hundred products, unless you sell 99 of them right over the course of a year, you will have 1 product left on the 366th day. That one product (remember, Amazon dates everything thoroughly) will incur a long-term storage fee. If you order another 100 products and they land in the USA on the 364th day, they're not going to charge storage fees until a year after that.

So you need to be careful about it. Never leave your products at Amazon fulfillment centers for more than a year. Even if you go over 1-year by 1 day, you have to pay a hefty fee! You never want to have products for more than a year. You also don't really want to have an unnecessary number of products because you get charged for inventory storage.

There's an inherent risk with any type of online business. You don't want to order 5 years' worth of products. You don't want to order a year's worth, even though that's too much. You don't know if you will be able to sell all of them within a year.

The sweet spot is ordering 90 days of inventory for a couple of reasons, but most importantly, because you don't want to order too little and you don't want to order too much. What I mean is that you don't want to order too little, which means it generally takes about 90 days for your products to be manufactured.

The product is created in a factory in China and then shipped via the ocean (which is the cheapest form of shipping) to a US Amazon fulfillment center. Especially the first time, it takes more time. You can make that a lot shorter. You can make it 60 days or make it 45 days for your next orders. The first order generally takes about 90 days.

If you ship via air, you can get your products much faster within 7 to 14 days, depending on how fast the manufacturer can make your products. But 90 days is like the most conservative estimate. So how do you do inventory forecasting? The hard way, and the better way. The best way is to add all of the top competitors.

Ignore the sponsored products and choose five of the best-selling products.

Use a spreadsheet and observe these products for five days. Do you know how many of them are sold every day? Everyday, you will notice how many are left. So you notice all the products and how many they are selling each day. After three days, you will get a basic idea of the number of products that are being sold each day. Then you multiply that number by 90 to get a 90-day inventory forecast. You want to multiply that by 90 days of inventory. And this is how many products you want to order. And that's simple. That's simple inventory forecasting.

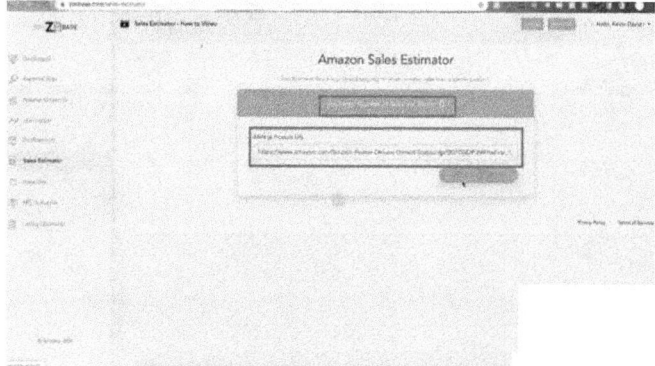

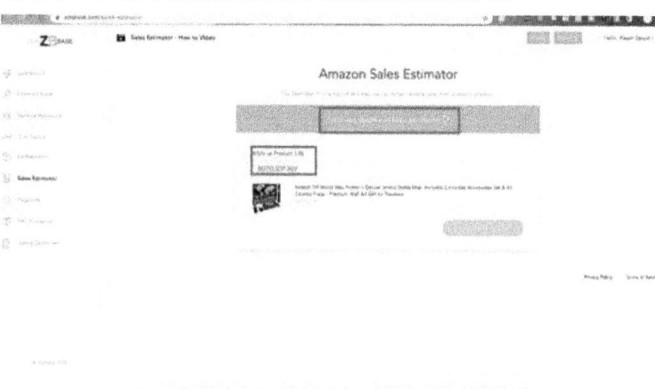

Now there is an easier way to do it. With the easier method, you put top-selling products on the Amazon sales estimator. Also, you can put the ASIN number in this calculator box to make things faster for you. For example, this one is selling for $788 per month. This one sells a lot, 3297.This one sells at 1230.

Now what I will do is to take out the two outliers from these five. 28 is an outlier, and 3200 is an outlier.

If we add these three up, it will be 788 + 1230 + 104. Divided by 3, the result is 707 per month. Now we have to divide 707 by 30 to get the daily sale. So it is about 23.5 units per day. So let's say 24 sales per day. Multiply 25 by 90 to get your inventory estimate. It is 2250.

Now, this is the easiest method to estimate. But ideally, you should use the first method, which is much harder but more accurate. Remember, there are nice tools available, such as Helium 10, Jungle Scout, but they will only give you an estimate. Instead of relying on tools, you should use the first method for inventory forecast. Remember, with the first method, you noted the sales of the top five products for three days.

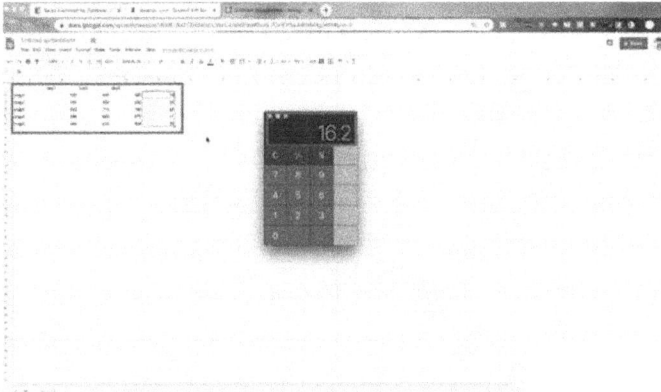

So now we are going to calculate them on a spreadsheet to get the average. The average comes to 16. So you need to multiply 16 by 90, which is 1440. This number is extremely accurate, and you should always follow this method when forecasting inventory.

Negotiate final price

Now, that we know exactly how many units we should need to keep a 90 day stock of inventory we need to talk about how to make sure that you're getting the cheapest price when buying your inventory. So why were we looking at this website? The reason is that this is the Chinese Alibaba, essentially. The address is www.1688.com.

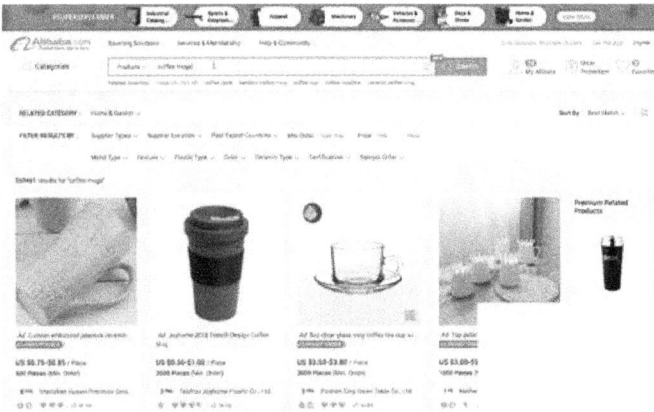

But first we are going to search for coffee mugs on Alibaba. This one is 98 cents. You will see a variety of prices. $80 cents, $90 cents, and so on. Obviously, when you actually message the manufacturers, most often they will say different prices. The price depends on a variety of things. .So what you are going to do is choose a coffee mug on 1688.com that is exactly or very similar to a coffee mug sold on AliBaba.com.

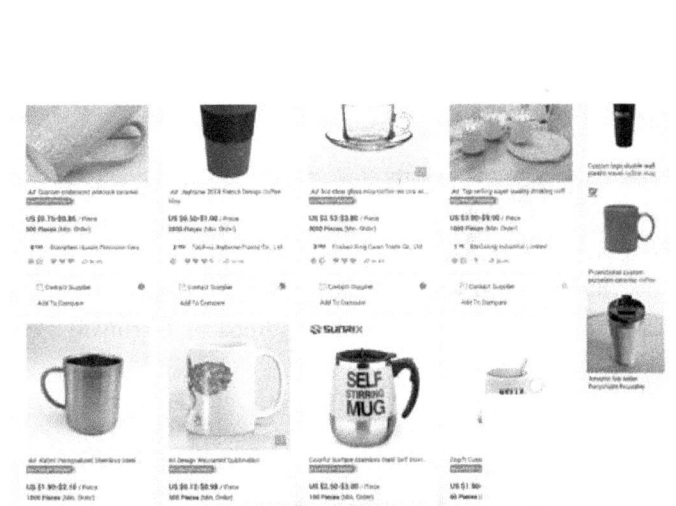

Go to WWW.1688.com and use Google translate to understand what the product descriptions are saying. Then type "coffee mugs" in the search box.

When checking the price, remember that 0.95 doesn't mean 95 cents. It actually symbolizes the Chinese currency, the Yuan. You can see the currency symbol on the left-hand side.

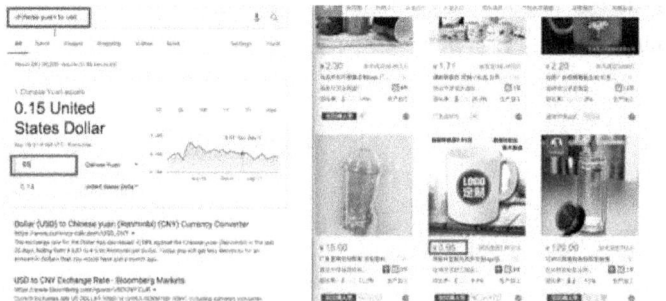

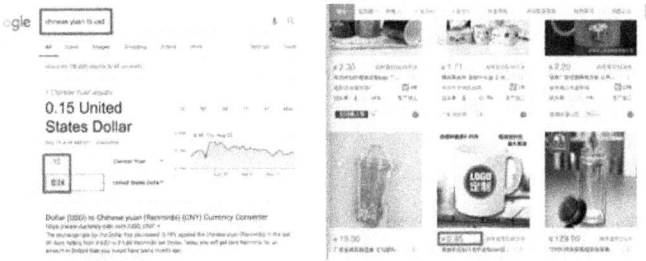

Use Google to convert Chinese currency to U.S. currency. When you calculate it, 95 yuan is actually $0.14 cents. Take a screenshot of the product from 1688.com and show it to your manufacturers on Alibaba. You can use the 1688 site to do research, but you can't actually buy products from this site because these manufacturers sell only to the domestic market. Take screenshots and then show them to your Alibaba manufacturers and tell them that these products are exactly like yours (or very similar), and they are selling at a fraction of your price.

The best way to get the lowest price from your Alibaba suppliers or manufacturers is to get at least three quotes from three completely different manufacturers. They should be separate companies, with different websites. Never get a price quote from only one manufacturer.   When you ask for quotes from three different manufacturers, you will get three different prices for your product. For example, one might say $3 per coffee mug, the second one might say $2 per coffee mug, and the third one might say $1 per coffee mug. Then go to the manufacturers who said a higher price and say that you have got 1 manufacturer who is saying $1 per coffee mug, so can you do it for $.90?

This is a nice way to get the best price from your manufacturers. Also, when you are asking for three quotes from three different manufacturers, ask for official quotes in their company form.

CAO COUNTY YU GUANG CRAFTS CO., LTD

NO.16 YaLuJiang Road Cao County Shandong Province China

Email: jackfan@yuguangcrafts.cn   Tel: +86 13793003746

Proforma Invoice

To: Aim2Trade

Address:83 Ridgedale Road Silverdale Auckland 0932 New Zealand
Tel: + 1 8017507932

Date:28th November 2016

P/I NO.:796928603183O3

Poduct Photo	Material	Size	Edge	Logo	QTY(PCS)	Unit Price(FOB Qingdao Port) (USD)	Amount USD
*c	bamboo	1)top wooden tray:20.4*3cm 2)bottom wooden tray:30*3cm 3)black silk print logo 4)lazy susan on bottom	Round	black silk print	250 pcs	US$ 11.6/pcs	$2,900
		the balance					$1,525.00

SAY USD:

Seller: Buyer: Aim2Trade

CAOXIAN ZHONGYI WOODEN CO.,LTD.

INDUSTRY PARK, ZHENGZHUANG, CAO COUNTY SHANDONG, CHINA

Contact Person: Aimee Hou

Tel:+(86)133-9621-2256

Fax 0088-530-8122 566

形式发票

Proforma Invoice   编号

NO : ZY-Aimee170901

DATE Sep 1 2017

SOLD TO:

Aim2Trade
83 Ridgedale Road
Silverdale Auckland 0932 New Zealand
Tel: 021 45 0927

唛头及号码 MARKS & NOS	(1) 货物名称 Description of Goods	(2)型号 Item	(2) 数量 Quantity	(3) 单价 Unit Price per set	(4) 总值 Total Amount($)
	bamboo tray		1000sets	$10.31	$10,310.00
	TOTAL:				$10,310.00

Bank Information:

Bank: Bank Of China Caoxian Sub-branch
Bank Add:East Gongye Road Caoxian County,Shandong Prov.,P.R.China
Swift:BKCHCNBJ500
Tel:0086-530-3227395
Beneficiary Name:Caoxian Zhongyi Wooden Co.,Ltd
Account No.: 2247 0397 5790
Tel 0086-530-8122068

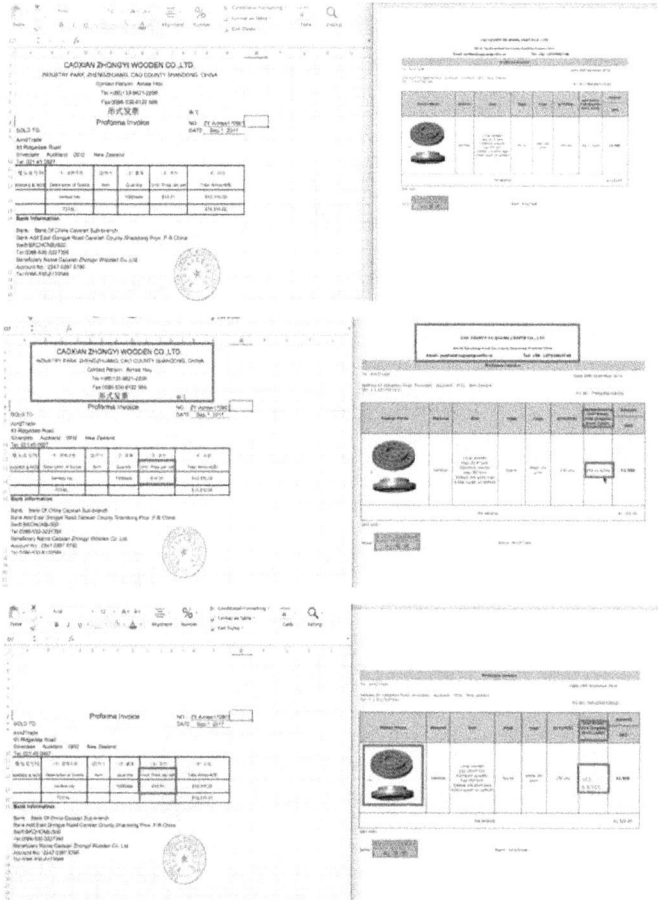

Here is one example of an official quote: These quotes are for essential oils. You can see it in one quote; it says 11.60 apiece and 10.31 apiece. To get the best price from your Alibaba manufacturer, show the lowest priced invoice to the higher priced manufacturer. Remember, keep the company addresses hidden on your invoice so the competitors do not know each other.

You can even manipulate the invoices and change the prices and send them to a higher price demanding manufacturer to get a better deal. When negotiating with manufacturers, use the FBA calculator to know your profit margin. For example, calculate what your buying price should be to get a 50% profit margin, and so on.

This is how you use your manufacturers and get the lowest price this way. Going to the 1688.com site, knowing the actual price of products and then showing invoices from one manufacturer to another manufacturer will give you leverage with your other manufacturers, which will ensure that you get the lowest price when buying your products. By leveraging the quotes of other manufacturers as well as 1688 you should be able to negotiate yourself the lowest price possible which will give you lots of advantage when trying to make profit when we begin selling

How to pay your Alibaba supplier

Now, I'm going to share with you how to pay your Chinese supplier on Alibaba. Alibaba is the biggest company in the world to purchase products in bulk, and it deals more with large quantities of products. On Alibaba, you can find suppliers to buy products in bulk to sell under your own brand on Amazon.

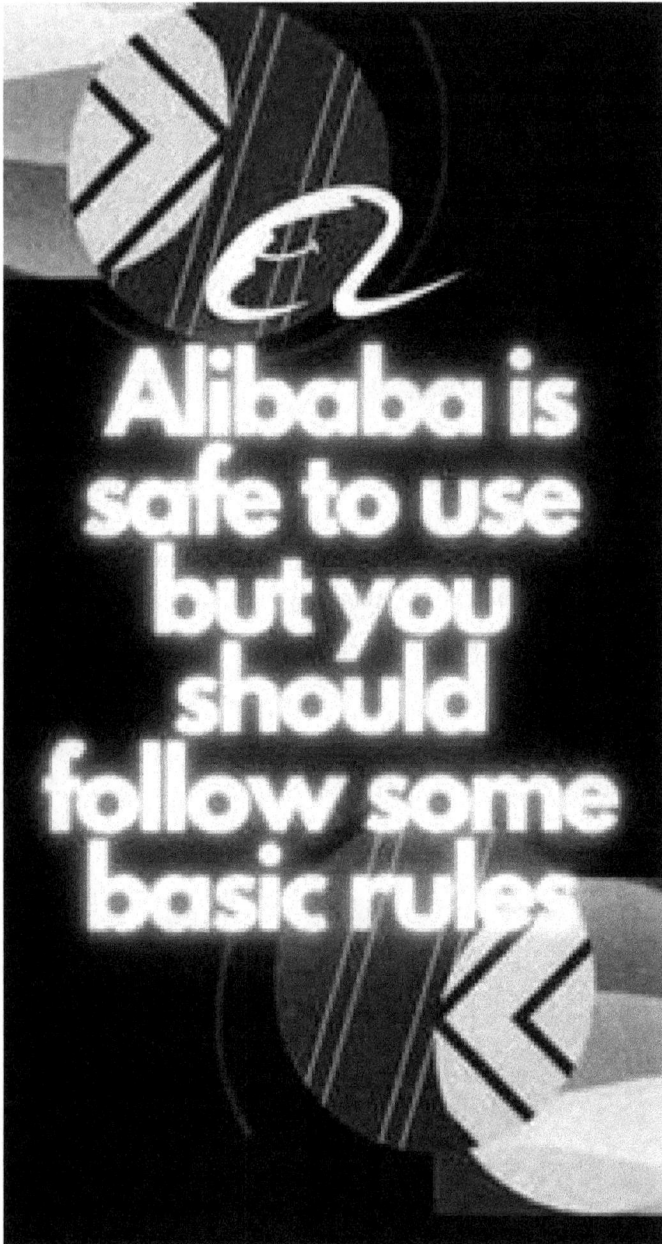

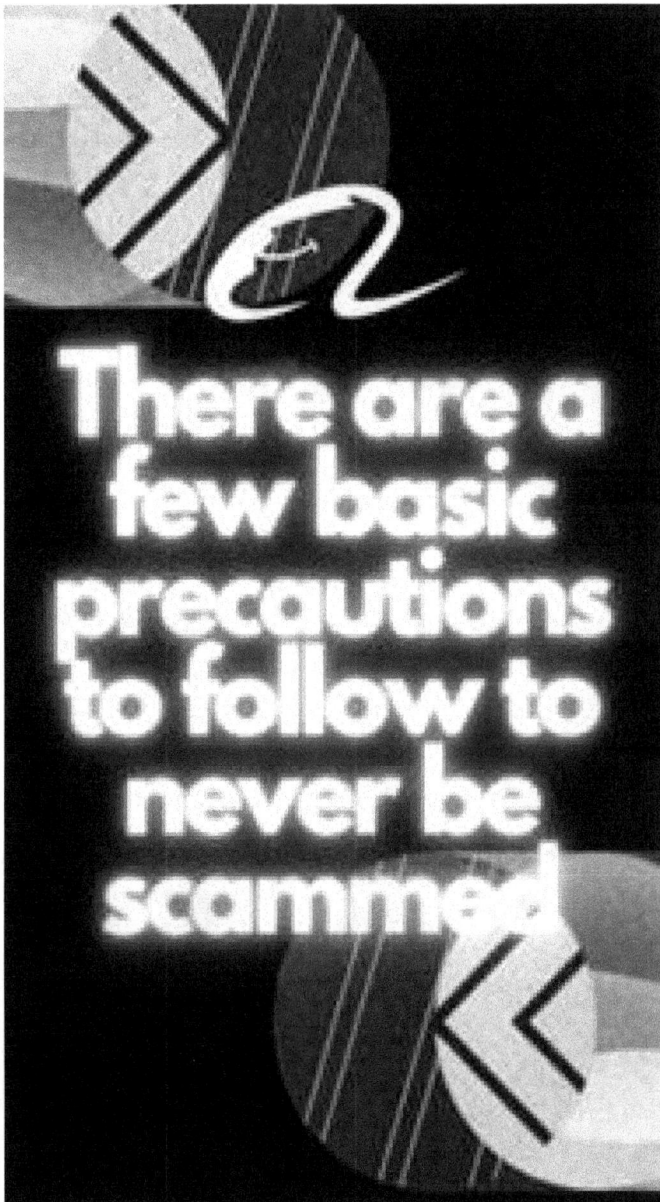

There are a few basic precautions to follow to never be scammed

Alibaba is a safe place to do business, but you should follow some general rules when dealing with Alibaba manufacturers. I've ordered more than $205,000 from different suppliers. And to be honest, I never really had that experience because there are a few basic precautions to follow to ensure you are never scammed on Alibaba.

1. Buy only from verified suppliers

2. Order only from Chinese companies

3. If you're paying with a wire transfer, make sure that the beneficiary name matches the company name

My first rule is to make sure that you only buy from verified suppliers. Make sure you order only from Chinese companies, and if you're paying by wire transfer, make sure that the beneficiary name matches the company name.

4. If your order is under $5000 use Alibaba's Trade Assurance.

They guarantee that your items will be shipped.

Service Types

If you order under $5,000, I highly recommend using Alibaba's "straight assurance" because it guarantees that your items will be shipped. If you want more protection, you can add Alibaba's Inspection Services as well. Another important piece of advice is to never pay a hundred percent of your invoice up front. Pay 30% at the beginning and pay the remaining 70% after the product has been manufactured and your inspector has come to make sure that the product meets the quality you were expecting. If the product gets inspected and it's to low of a quality to bring to market you can work with your manufacturer to get the product reproduced or find a new manufacturer. If you paid all 100% of the product price at once you are at much greater risk of the manufacturer running off with your money or if the product is low quality you might have your manufacturer redoing the order at a high quality.

Processing Time and Fees

⚠ For various tasks between US-based buyers and US-based suppliers, Alibaba.com currently only supports credit/debit card payments, and the processing time is approximately 2 hours.

Payment Method	Currency/Limit	Transaction Fee	Processing Time
Credit/Debit Card	multi-currency	2.99% of payment amount	1 - 2 hours
PayPal	multi-currency	2.99% of payment amount	1 - 2 hours
Apple Pay	multi-currency	2.99% of payment amount	1 - 2 hours
Google Pay	multi-currency	2.99% of payment amount	1 - 2 hours
Wire Transfer	multi-currency	around $40	3 - 7 business day
Wire Transfer	local currency	around 1 cent of local currency	1 - 3 business day

Processing Time and Fees

Payment Method	Currency/Limit	Transaction Fee	Processing Time
Credit/Debit Card	multi-currency	2.99% of payment amount	1 - 2 hours

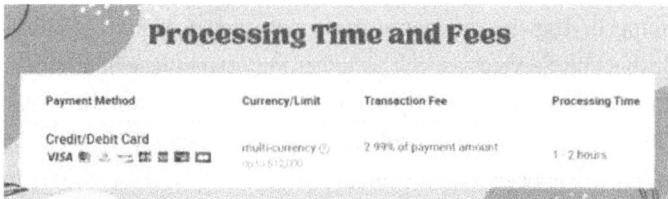

You can pay online, you can directly pay with your credit card, or you can pay by wire transfer. You can use pay later as well if you are a U.S. buyer. And finally, there are some other options, like PayPal and E-Checking.

Processing Time and Fees

Payment Method	Currency/Limit	Transaction Fee	Processing Time
Apple Pay	multi-currency	2.99% of payment amount	1 - 2 hours
Google Pay	multi-currency	2.99% of payment amount	1 - 2 hours

Recently, they started accepting Google Pay and Apple Pay as well. Check each payment method to see the processing fees and transaction time before using it.

5.

Wire Transfer

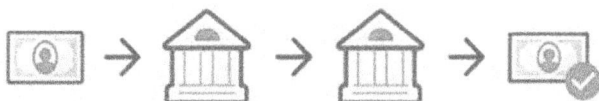

The first option to pay your supplier is a credit or debit card. As you can see, they accept Visa, Mastercard, American Express, and the rest of these companies. They support more than 20 currencies, like US dollars, Canadian dollars, and so on, which enables you to pay up to $12,000 per transaction. The transaction fee is 3%, and the processing time is 1 to 2 hours.

Payment Method	Currency/Limit	Transaction Fee	Processing Time
Credit/Debit Card VISA	multi currency up to $12,000	2.99% of payment amount	1 - 2 hours

The next payment method is PayPal, which, to be honest, most Chinese suppliers don't like a lot. Usually they ask you to pay with a wire transfer, but you have all these options available to you. Pay with whichever method suits you. With PayPal, you have the same currency options, a $12,000 limit, and a 3% transaction fee. And it is going to take one to two hours as well. It has been a few months since Alibaba started accepting Apple Pay and Google Pay. They are both convenient methods of payment to use, and they both accept different currencies. They have the same 3% transaction fee and a 1 to 2-hour processing fee. Currently, Google Pay has a limit of $500, which is almost nothing for an order from China. Hopefully, they will increase the limit soon.

Finally, the last option for large payments of more than $5,000 is to use a wire transfer. With wire transfers, there's always a $40 transaction fee, and some banks have lower transaction fees. For example, at RBC Bank in Canada, the fee is $15 to $20, but sometimes fees go up. In some banks, the fee is a bit higher. The processing time is two to seven business days, but usually it takes only 24 hours.

They accept multi-currency and there is no limit on that, which means if you want to pay $100,000 or millions of dollars to your supplier, this is the best option to transfer your money. Now, let's discuss how you can communicate with your supplier on Alibaba. To avoid scams, do not do transactions outside of the Alibaba platform. If you use an outside method to communicate with your supplier, then Alibaba won't guarantee a meditation process or refund. Use Alibaba chat. It is safe compared to other platforms, and you can chat on your phone as well.

Alibaba Production Monitoring & Inspection Services

Now we are going to discuss two services that Alibaba offers.

The first one is product monitoring services, and the second one is inspection services. When you know these two services well, you will know which inspection service will work best for you.

You need to use these services for your Amazon customers to get their products in perfect condition. You will get more positive reviews and avoid negative ones.

Now I am going to discuss four rules so you can avoid wasting your time, money, and getting negative reviews from your Amazon clients.

1. Always tell your supplier right from the beginning that you're going to hire an inspector.

First rule: Always tell your supplier at the beginning that you are going to hire an inspector. This way, your Alibaba suppliers will know that they can't use low-quality materials to produce your products.

2. Never work with suppliers who don't accept inspections.

The second rule is to never work with suppliers who don't accept inspections. If a supplier says that they don't accept inspections, then find another supplier.

3. Have a firm purchase invoice

The third rule is to have a firm purchase invoice. For example, if you mentioned 3000 pieces of one product, then stay firm on that number even if the supplier insists that you buy more.

4. Withhold a percentage of your payment until the goods are ready & inspection takes place.

Fourth rule: Withhold a percentage of your payment until the goods are ready and an inspection takes place.

Never pay 100% of the payment upfront. Pay 30% as a deposit and 70% when your products are ready. A few times, I paid 100% upfront and regretted it every time.

Your supplier will respond to you quickly if you pay them in installments.

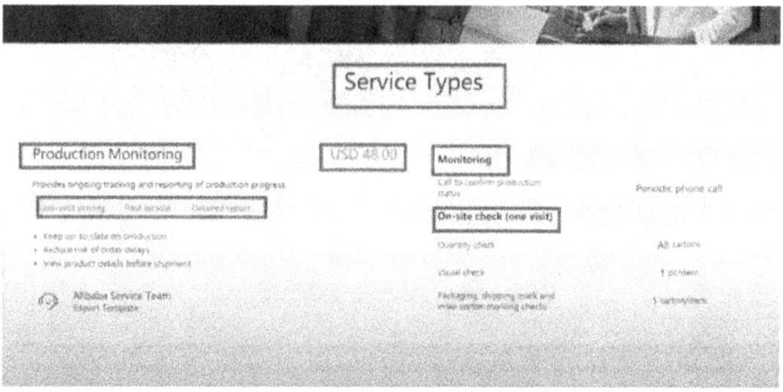

Service Types

Generally, Alibaba provides two types of services: production monitoring and inspection. Production monitoring provides reporting of production progress. The second one is inspection services.

First, let's talk about production monitoring.

Most Amazon sellers use this service because it is cheap and only costs $48. This package includes:

· Call to confirm production status.

· Periodic phone calls

· Quantity check

· Visual check

· Packaging Check

Here is an example of a production monitoring report. As you can see, it includes general information about the supplier and buyer, a planned finish date, and an actual finish date.

In the lower part of the report, you can see the overall result summary, which includes quantity, packing, shipping mark, additional items, and remarks.

The next section discusses the details. It includes the order quantity and the actual quantity.

The next section includes photos. Here you will see the actual pictures of your products.

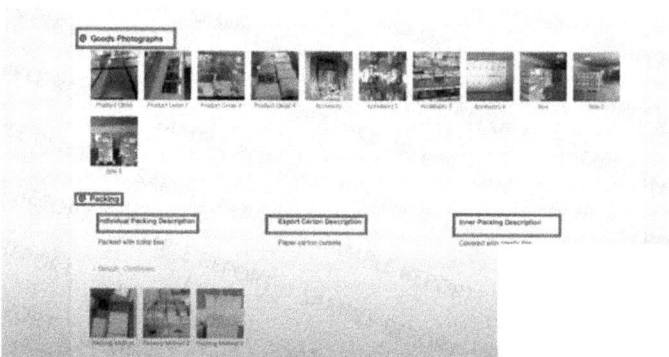

Next are packing details and some real pictures of them.

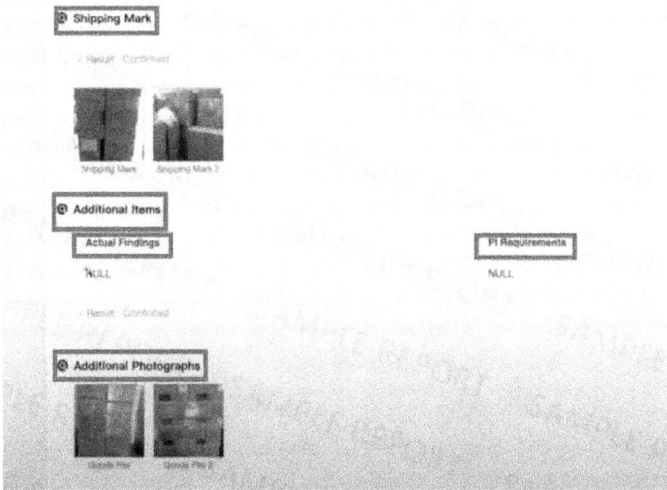

Next is the shipping mark, and finally, additional items.

The next service Alibaba provides is the inspection service. It starts at $118 and goes up as high as $220. Using third-party services will cost you more.

Here are three third-party service providers that Alibaba works with. They are: Bureau Veritas, China Certification & Inspection Group and SGS.

Now take a look at an inspection report.

Here is an inspection report from Bureau Veritas. It includes more than nine pages of detailed results. The first section contains general information and a summary of the overall results.

| 5. | **On-Site Test** (Details in Section E) | | x | | C.6 |

C. REMARKS

1.	No approval sample or reference sample or client product picture was available for this inspection.
2.	No information to compare the shipping mark & all artwork.
3.	No purchase order number, item number or client name information was presented on product or product package, so inspector could not verify if the products inspected were the client ordered.
4.	The factory provided PI for reference.
5.	There was not quantity information on the Trade Assurance platform, and the quantity counting was based on the packing list provided by factory.
6.	Found no suitable equipment to do Metal Detection Test for component pillow, but the factory provided Metal Detection Test record on site.

D. WORKMANSHIP (Basic Function & Appearance)

Inspection Standard	ANSI/ASQ Z1.4 (formerly known as MIL-STD-105E)						
Inspection Level - Workmanship / Visual:	S-3	Acceptance Quality Limit(AQL) - Critical Defectives:				Not Allowed	
Sampling Plan - Workmanship / Visual:	Single / Normal		AQL - Major Defectives:			2.5	
			AQL - Minor Defectives:			4.0	
Sample Size - Workmanship / Visual:	Critical	13	Major	5	Minor	13	
Defect Code	Defect Description*				Critical	Major	Minor
	Untrimmed thread end(4cm)				0	0	1
		Total Found:			0	0	1
		Accept:			0	0	1
		Result:				PASS	

E. ON SITE TEST

	INSPECTION PROPERTY	FINDING
1.	Barcode verification	PASS
2.	Carton dimension measurement	PACK 20:13.45KG/4 PACK 25:16.71KG/4 PASS

* For Hardline & E&E Products

X   SIGNATURES

	INSPECTION REPORT- Final Version THIS DOCUMENT IS NON-NEGOTIABLE		Client Name:	ABC Limited	
			Inspection No.:	1019197XXXX	
			Report Date:	22-Jul-2019	Page 3 of 9
Inspector Name:	Link Fang	Factory Representative Name:			
Signature:	Link Fang	Signature:			
Date and time:	2019-Jul-19	Date and time:			

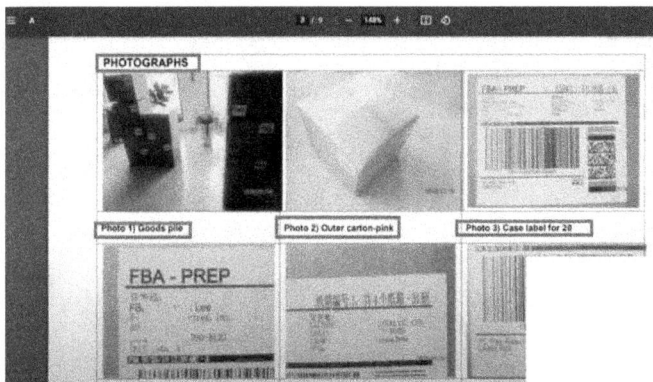

PHOTOGRAPHS

Photo 1) Goods pile · Photo 2) Outer carton-pink · Photo 3) Case label for 20

FBA - PREP

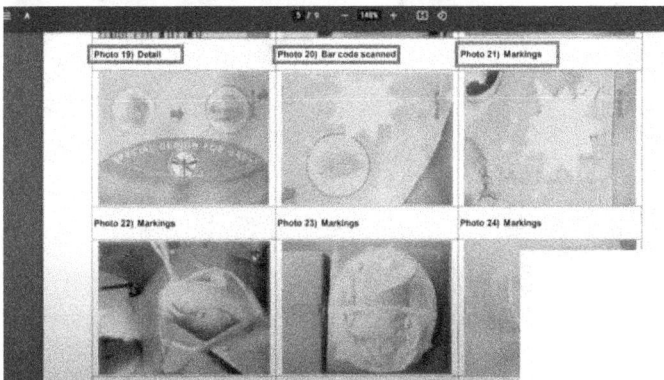

Photo 19) Detail · Photo 20) Bar code scanned · Photo 21) Markings

Photo 22) Markings · Photo 23) Markings · Photo 24) Markings

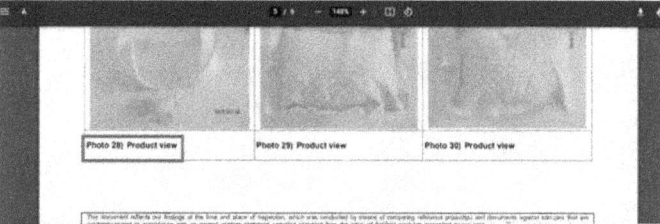

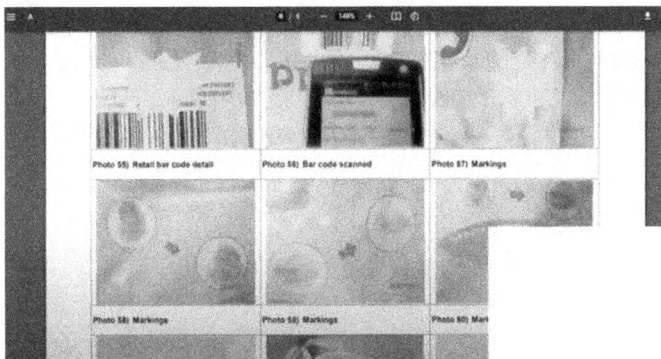

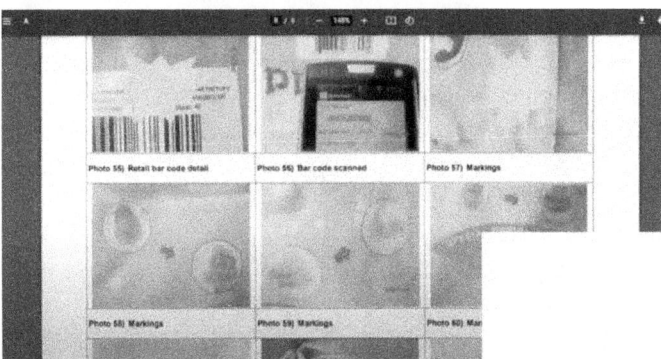

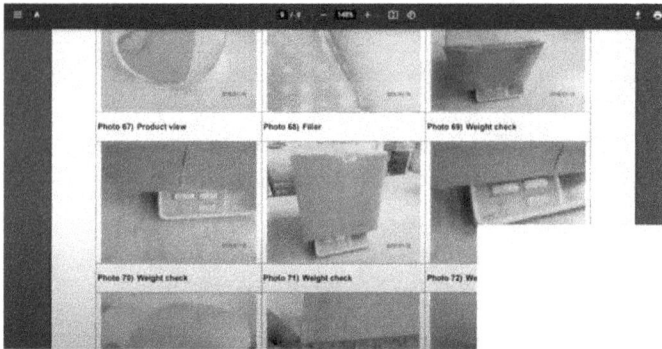

As you can see, this inspection report is extremely detailed when compared with a production monitoring report. In this report, you will get various high-quality photos, including the inspector's name and signature. On the last page of the report, it includes 75 high-quality reports, which is amazing.

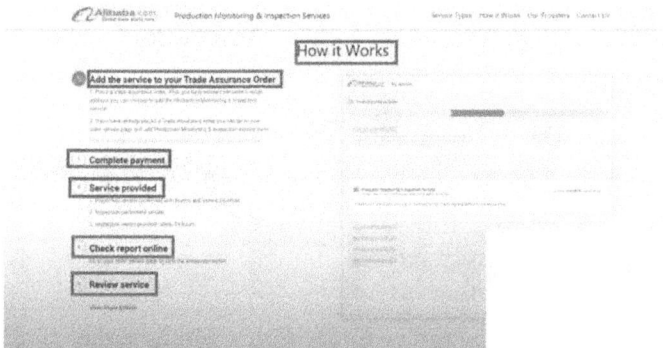

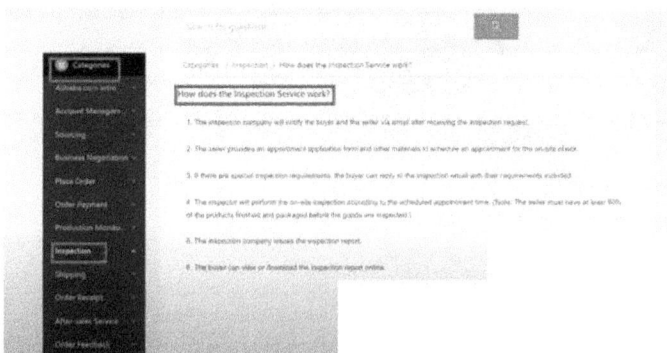

So how do you use these services from Alibaba?

Once you pay your fee for a production monitoring report, the inspection company will email you and the seller. Next, they will schedule a date for an on-site check. Then, when the seller finishes production, they will set an appointment time. Within 24 hours, the inspector uploads the final inspection report, so you can review and download the report from Alibaba.

Finding Your Freight Forwarder

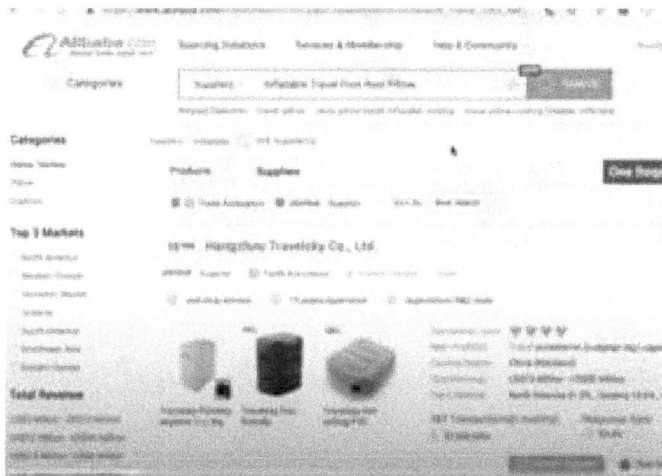

Now we are going to discuss how you can get your products from your manufacture's factory in China or other countries to an Amazon warehouse. We've already covered a few incoterms: EXW, FOB, DDU, and DDP.

If you sign a deal based on DDP, all the responsibility for shipping the product from the manufacturer's factory to Amazon's warehouse goes to the manufacturer. You can make other types of deals, such as FOB or EX-Works.

Let's say you made a deal with the manufacturer of the above image. Your manufacturer probably knows a freight forwarder who can ship your products to the Amazon warehouse. However, getting a freight forwarder from your manufacturer might cost you more. So you can choose your own freight forwarder.

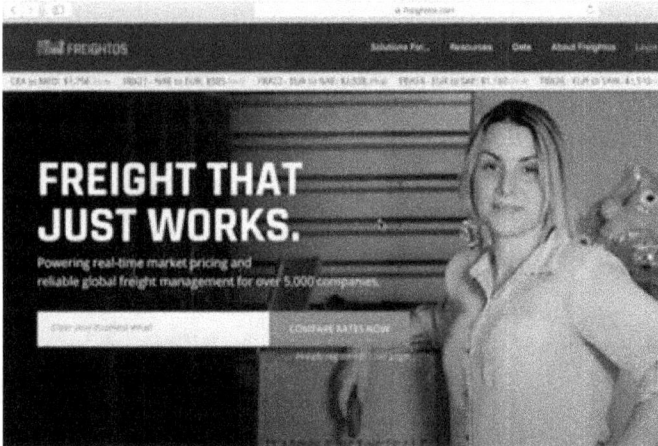

Or you can find your own freight forwarder on the FREIGHTOS website. There are also other similar sites available on the internet.

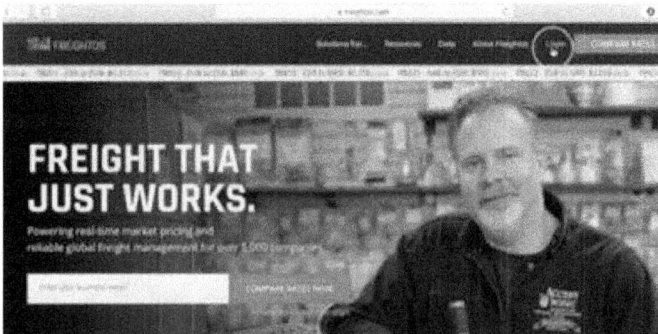

First, log in to the FREIGHTOS site. You can sign up easily with an email address.

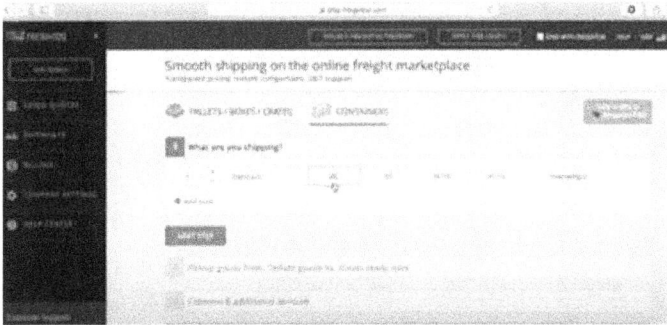

Once you log in, you will see this screen. You need to fill in the blanks according to your product. But before that, you need to do something else.

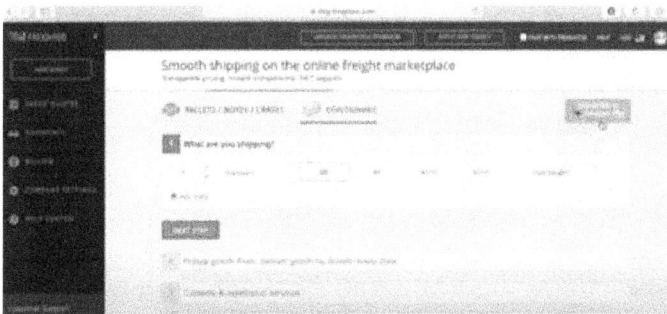

In the top right-hand corner, there is a sign that says "click to ship to Amazon FBA". Click it because this is what you are searching for. Here you will find freight forwarders to deliver your products to Amazon's warehouse.

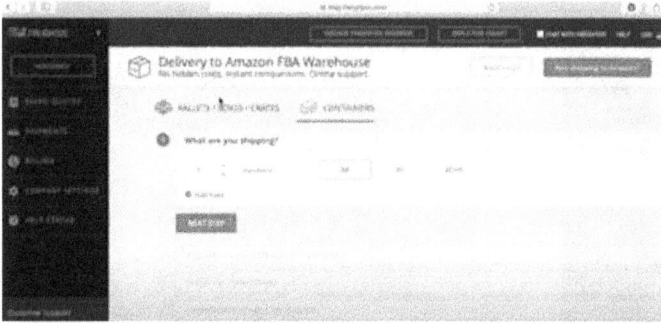

On this page, there are two options. Which type of packing are you using to package your products? Either pallets or containers.

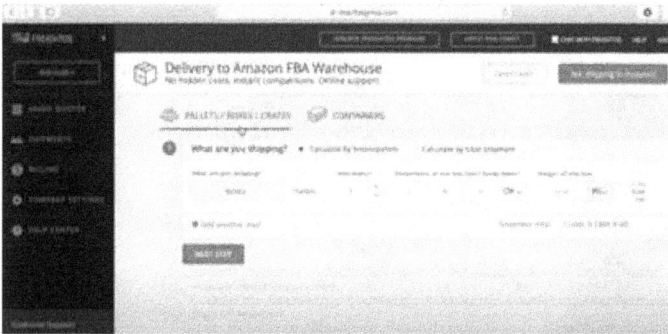

We are choosing pallet boxes on the left because we want boxes.

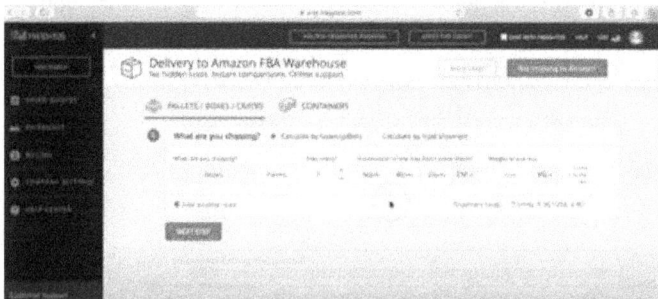

Now fill in the blanks about the boxes. You can only choose a predetermined size and weight for the boxes. So you can't choose heavier or oversize boxes. 23 kilograms for each box.

The current section only allows you to choose boxes that are a certain size and weight.

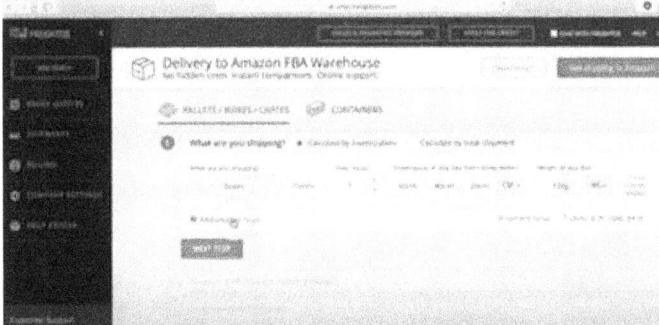

To add another type of box, click "Add another load".

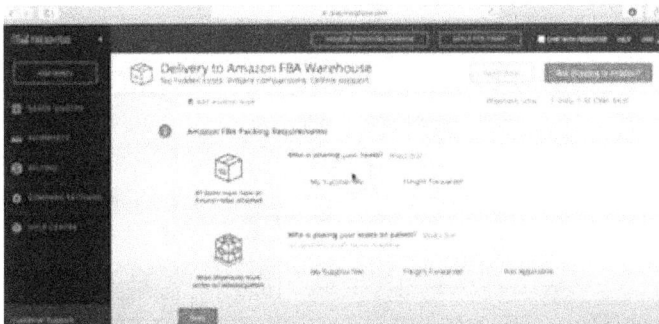

Now fill in the blanks.

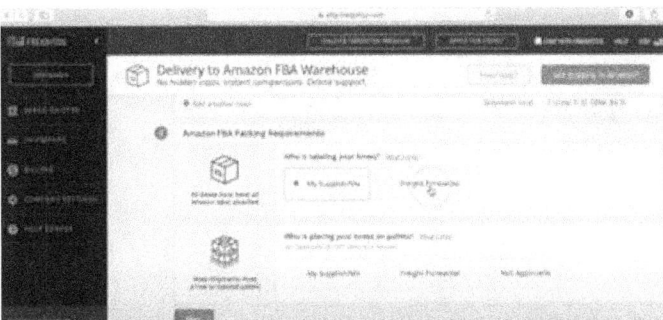

The next question is, "who is labeling your boxes?" Choose the "My Supplier/Me" option. Amazon provides you with two types of labels. One for attaching to the product and another for attaching to the product boxes. Amazon will scan the labels and sort them accordingly.

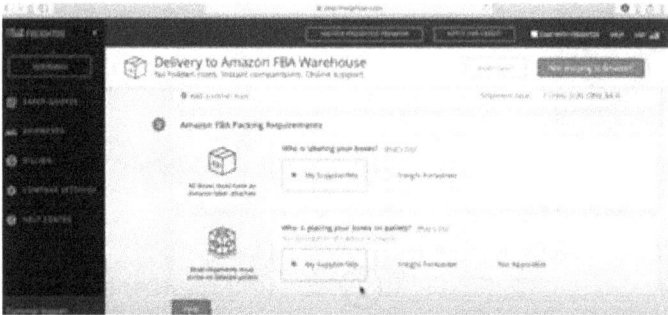

Now fill in the blanks. If you choose a freight forwarder, they will charge an extra fee for it. The next question is, "Who is placing your boxes on pallets?" Ideally, your supplier should do this. If you choose a freight forwarder, you have to pay a higher fee. Then click "next."

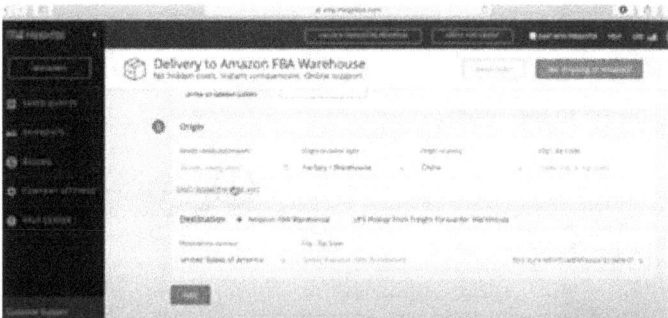

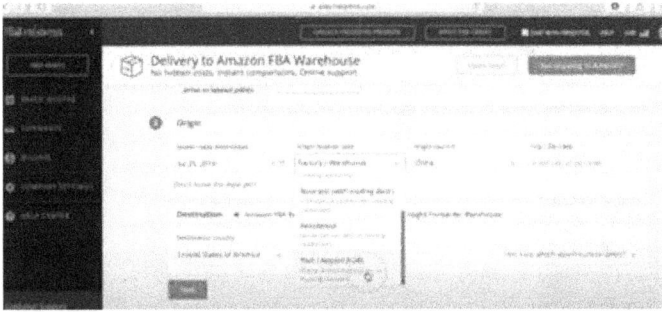

Here you have to describe where the freight forwarder should ship your products. Fill in the form. Here I chose China because you will usually use a Chinese manufacturer.

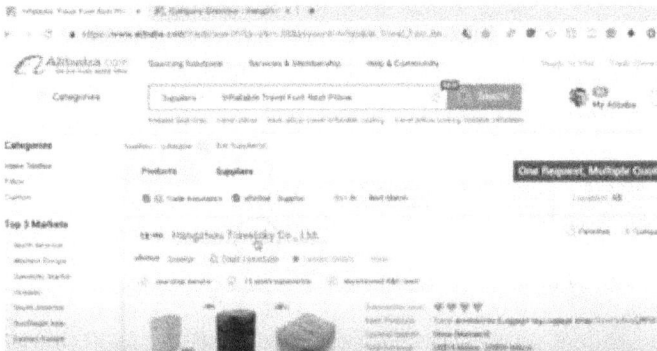

Your manufacturer will give you his factory address.

Also, you can find information about your manufacturer from the manufacturer's Alibaba profile page.

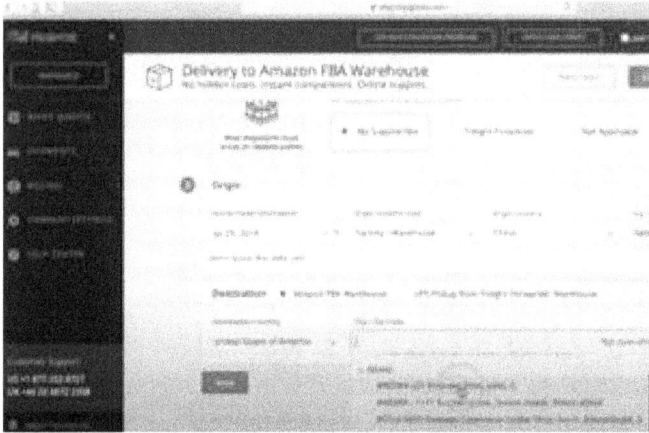

Now that we set up our shipping we need the labels for final delivery into amazon. As you can see, you can send your products to a variety of Amazon warehouses. Choose your destination and then click next.

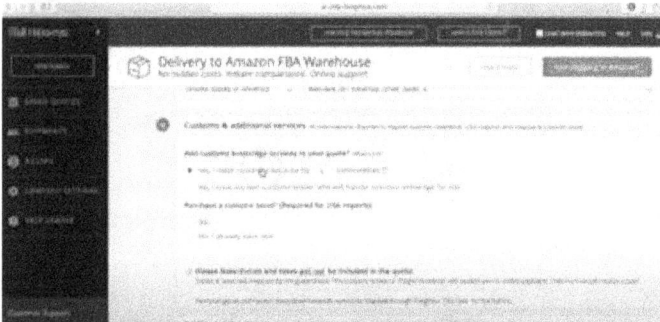

On the next page, you need to fill in some information about customs. In the beginning, you will not have your own brokerage service, so choose the above one. Actually, your freight forwarder will deal with the customs formalities. If you are buying only one type of product, then choose one here. If more than one, then choose another number.

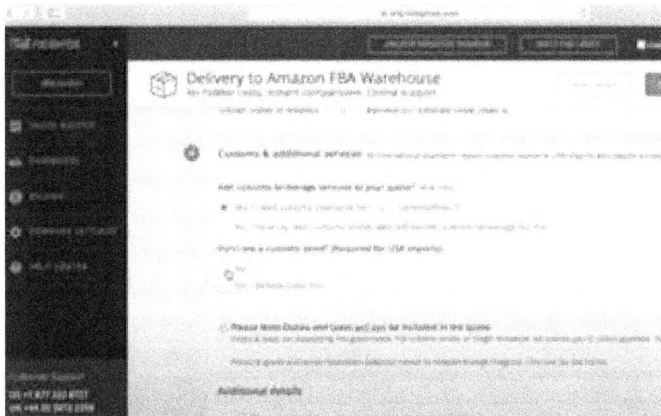

There is a customs bond. Click "yes."

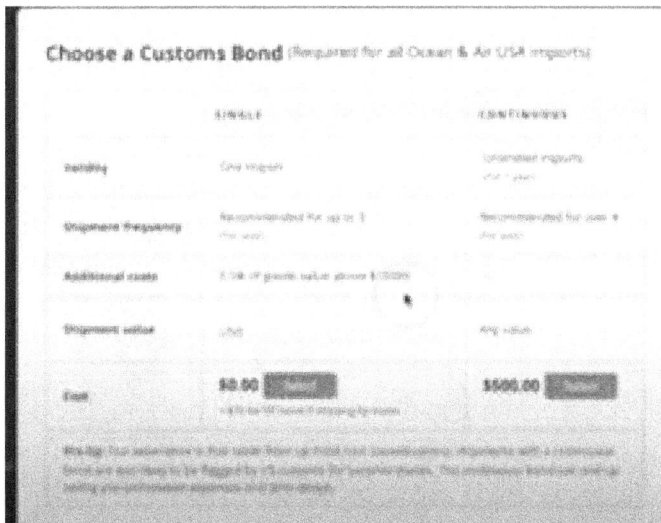

Then you will see a price table.

For a shipment of $1000, you pay $50. If you send it on a sea route fee is $75.

You can deal with it by talking with the freight forwarder because they already have an annual plan like the right part of the price table. Make a deal with your freight forwarder so you don't have to pay a fee each time you import your products.

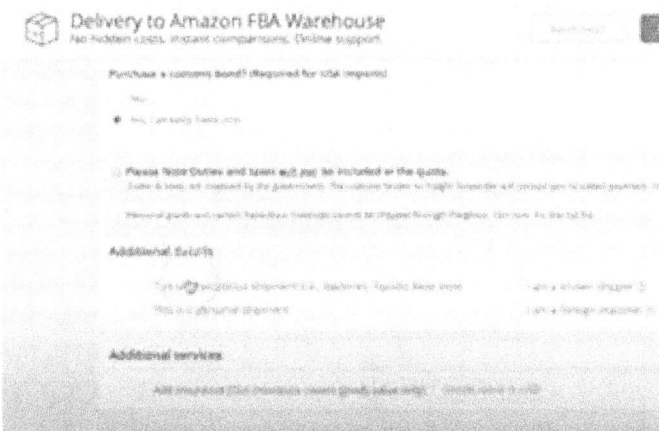

Now go below. Here in the additional details, it says, "This is a hazardous shipment."

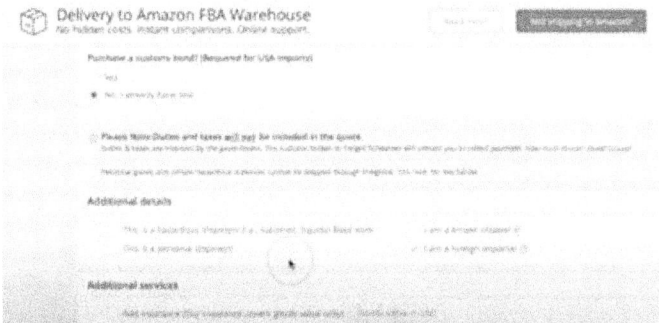

Only mark "I am a foreign importer" and keep the rest blank.

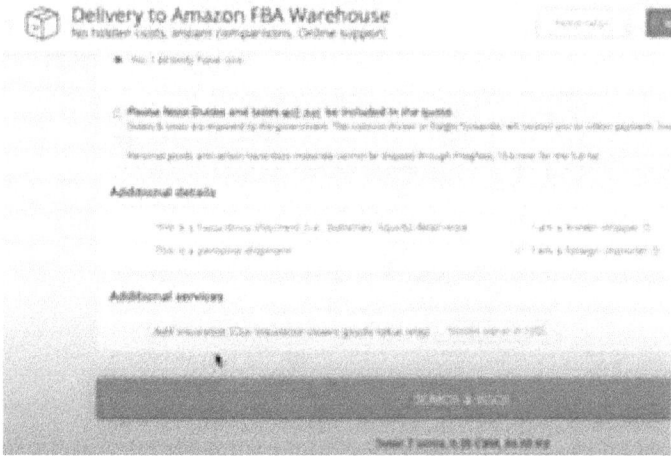

Now go to "additional services".

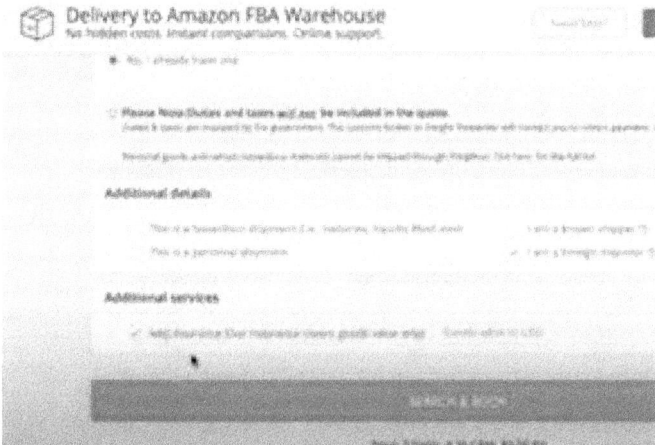

It includes insurance. If you want insurance for your products, make sure you add insurance.

Then click "Search & Book." Now the system will show you a list of freight forwarders.

As you can see, there are 111 results, which means you get 111 different price offers.

You can choose "Express, Ocean, or Air".

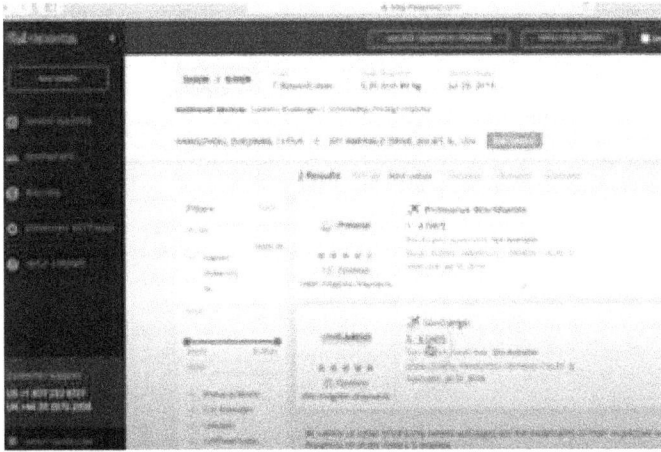

For example, some of the express service providers are offering 1 to 4 days or 3 to 6 days, and prices are also different.

Now let's have a look at the ocean ones. Click on the "cheapest" section. Now you can see the cheapest ones.

The cheapest one is $585. The list also shows how many days it will take to ship your products. So the form gives you an idea of the price and time.

Now, look at air shipping. The cheapest one is $858, and it will take them 21 to 26 days.

To avoid running out of stock, you may sometimes have to choose fast and express shipping. So you have several options here: express, ocean, air, cheapest, quickest, and greenest.

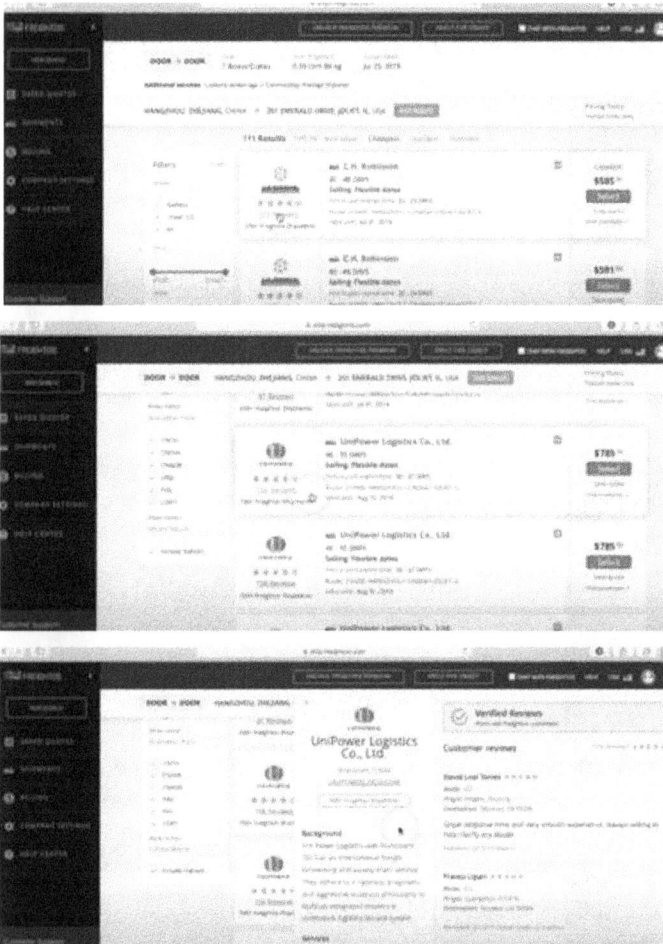

Each freight forwarder has reviews from their previous clients. So read the reviews to learn more about them. I especially read the negative reviews. Get a price estimate from the FREIGHTOS site, then tell your manufacturer that you have a freight forwarder who is taking $850, and see if the manufacturer's freight forwarder will agree to the same price or not. Choosing a manufacturer's freight forwarder gives you some added advantages because they know each other, so things will go smoothly. But if your manufacturer's freight forwarder asks for a higher price, then choose one from the FREIGHTOS site.

There is one important thing I want you to say: if possible, get your products from Europe. The same amount of product imported from Europe costs only $300 and takes 3 to 6 days. But if you want to import it from China, it will take 40+ days and cost around $800. The reason is that almost all the products from Europe use air shipment

How to ship your products to an Amazon Warehouse

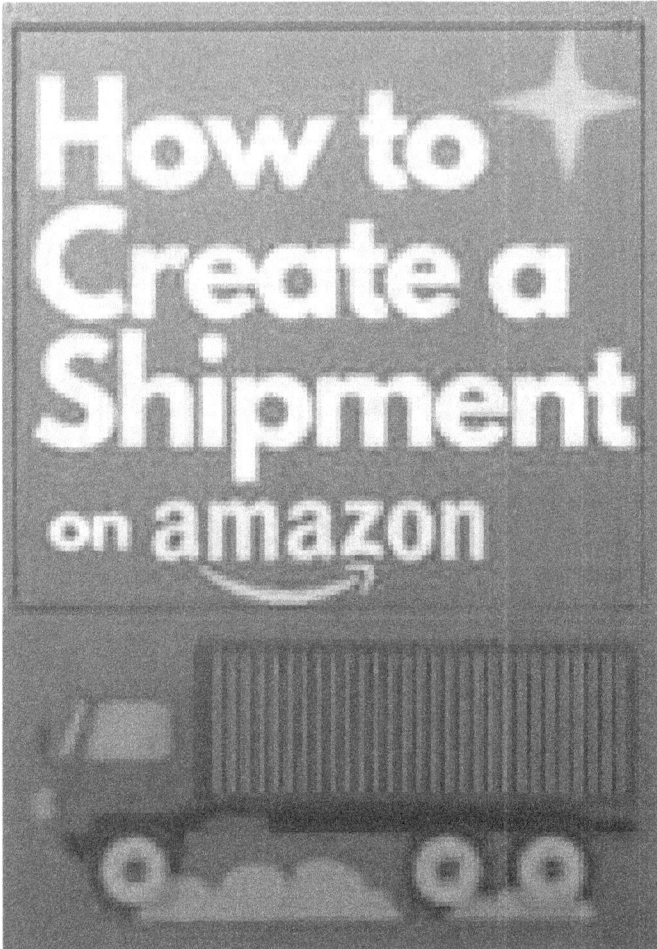

How to Create a Shipment on amazon

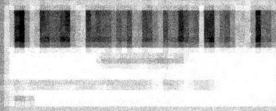

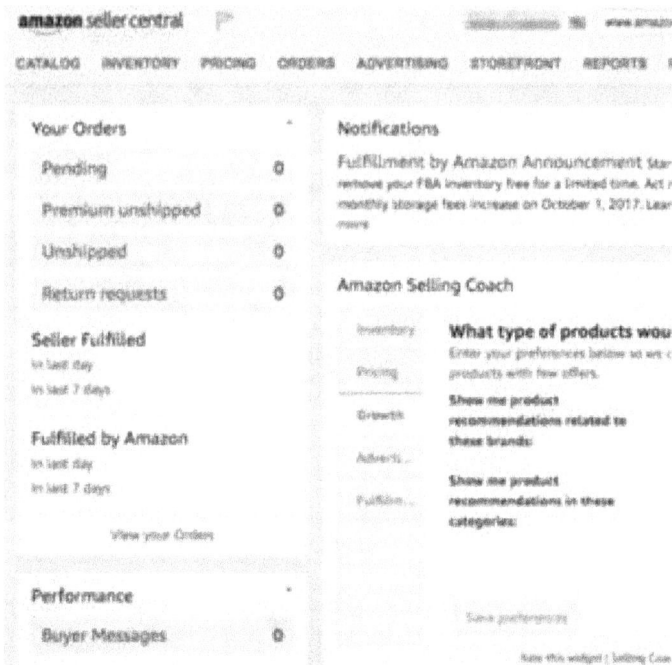

How to ship your products to an Amazon Warehouse

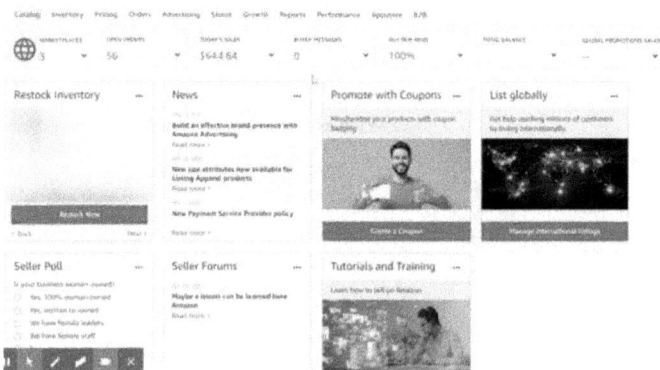

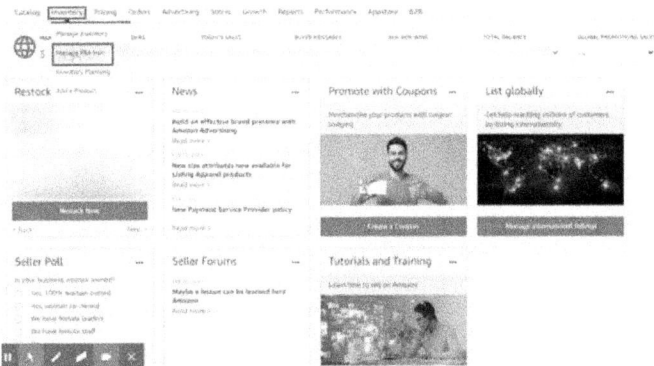

First, you need to go to your seller's central panel. Click "Inventory" and then "Manage FBA Inventory."

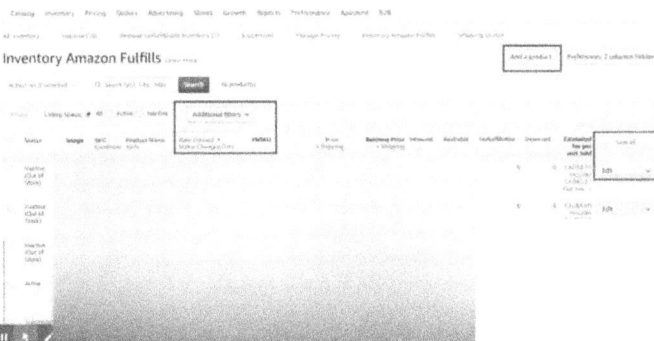

Before this, first, make sure you add your products by using "Add product."

Then you need to click "Edit" over here and select "Send/Replenish Inventory".

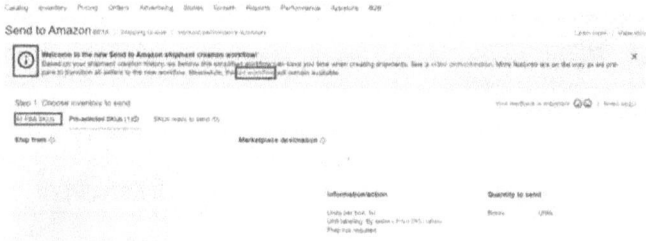

On the next screen, click "All FBA SKUs."

Then click "Create new packing template."

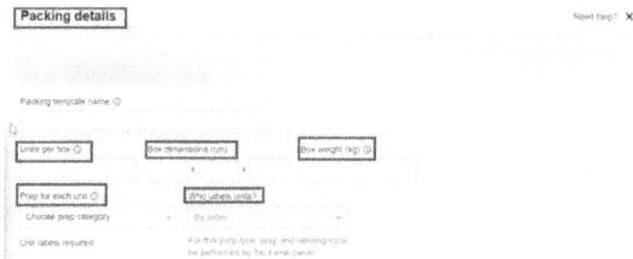

Packing details

Packing template name ⓘ

Units per box ⓘ   Box dimensions   Box weight (kg) ⓘ

x

Prep for each unit ⓘ   Who labels units?

Choose prep category   By seller

Unit labels required   For this prep type, prep and labeling must
be performed by the same owner

Packing details   Need help? ✕

Packing template name ⓘ

Product x - 50pcs/ctn

Units per box ⓘ   Box weight (kg) ⓘ

50   Many units require prep and   x 30
          labeling to be received
Prep for each unit ⓘ   correctly at the fulfillment
          centers. Any required prep and
Choose prep category   labeling must be applied to
          each sellable unit.
Unit labels required   Learn more.   type, prep and receiving must
          be performed by the same owner

Packing details   Need help? ✕

Choose prep category
Adult

Apparel, fabric, plush, and   ensions (cm)   Box weight (kg) ⓘ
textiles   x 40   x 30   12

Baby products   Who labels units?

Choose prep category   By seller

Unit labels required   For this prep type, prep and labeling must
          be performed by the same owner

Packing details

Packing template name
Product x - 50pcs/ctn

Units per box
50

Box dimensions (cm)
50   x 40   x 30

Box weight (kg)
12

Prep for each unit
No prep needed

Who labels units?
By se...

Prep not required
Unit labels required

For this prep type, prep and labeling must
be performed by the name owner.

Then fill out this form. Sometimes these forms ask for measurements in cm and kg. Other times, they ask for inches and pounds. Fill out the form according to you're the details given to you by your manufacturer.

Packing details

Packing template name
Product x - 50pcs/ctn

Units per box
50

Box dimensions (cm)
50   x 40   x 30

Box weight (kg)
12

Prep for each unit
No prep needed

Who labels units?
By seller

Prep not required
Unit labels required

For this prep type, prep and labeling must
be performed by the name owner.

Cancel   Save

Then click "Save."

on ⊙   Filter

                        Only show SKUs with case pack template

Information/action   Quantity to send

Units per box: 50   Boxes   Units
Unit labeling: By seller - Print SKU labels
Prep not required

Units per box: 50   Boxes   Units
Unit labeling: By seller - Print SKU labels
Prep not required

Packing template needed first

Units per box: 50   Boxes
Unit labeling: By seller - Print SKU labels
Prep not required

On the next page, you will see all your information. You can print SKU labels here.

on ⓘ

Filter

☐ Only show SKUs with case pack template

Information/action

Quantity to send

🖉 Units per box: 50
Unit labeling: By seller - Print SKU labels
Prep not required

Boxes   Units

🖉 Units per box: 50
Unit labeling: By seller - Print SKU labels
Prep not required

Boxes		Units
2 ⇕	=	100	⊗

Ready to send

Packing template needed first

Information/action

Quantity to send

🖉 Units per box: 50
Unit labeling: By seller - Print SKU labels
Prep not required

Boxes   Units

👁 Units per box: 50
Unit labeling: By seller - Print SKU labels
Prep not required

Boxes		Units	
2	=	100	Modify or remove

This product has a maximum inventory level and exceeds the allowed quantity. See the maximum inventory level on the Restock Inventory page. Learn more.

Information/action   Quantity to send

Units per box: 50   Boxes   Units
Unit labeling: By seller - Print SKU labels
Prep not required

Units per box: 50   ✓ Ready to send Modify or remove
Unit labeling: By seller - Print SKU labels   Boxes: 1
Prep not required   Units: 50

Packing template needed first

You can modify or remove your products whenever you want.

Information/action   Quantity to send

Units per box: 50   Boxes   Units
Unit labeling: By seller - Print SKU labels
Prep not required

Units per box: 50   Boxes   Units
Unit labeling: By seller - Print SKU labels   1   0   50
Prep not required
                                                 Ready to send

Packing template needed first

If you have everything ready, then click "Ready to send."

Preparing template needed first

‹ 1 ›

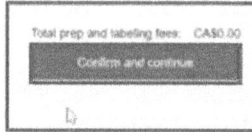

Start new   Go to Shipping Queue

Then scroll down and click "Confirm and continue."

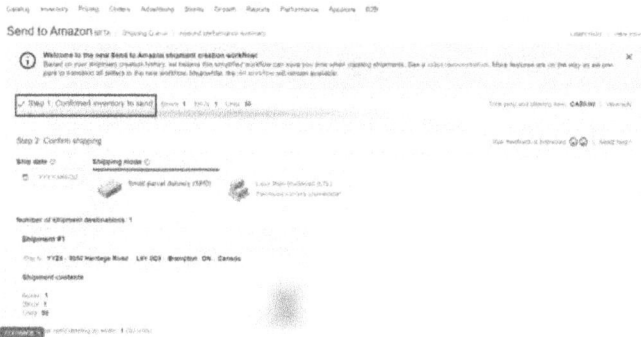

This was the first step, which included "confirmed inventory to send" and "address".

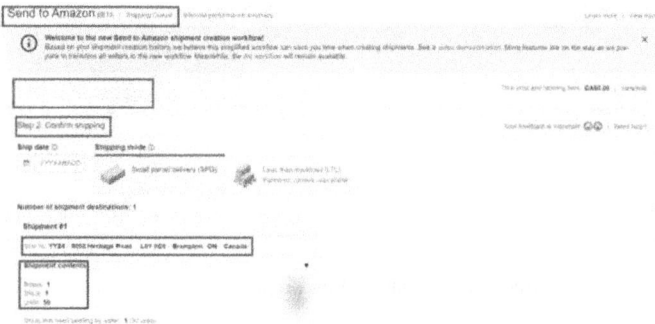

Now fill in the shipping form to confirm shipping.

Next, choose a shipping date.

Then choose the shipping mode.

Next, confirm your shipping address.

You can choose a "Non-Amazon partnered center." For example, you can choose FedEx, UPS, or others. Amazon gives you a discount through UPS. The price depends on the weight of your boxes and the distance of the shipment.

Then click "Accept charges and confirm shipping".

Next Amazon is going to give you shipping labels that you can attach to your cartoons or boxes.

So this description was based on the newer Amazon FBA beta version.

Now we are going to discuss the "Old Workflow" version.

So this is the old version.

You can select "Individual products" or "Case-packed products."

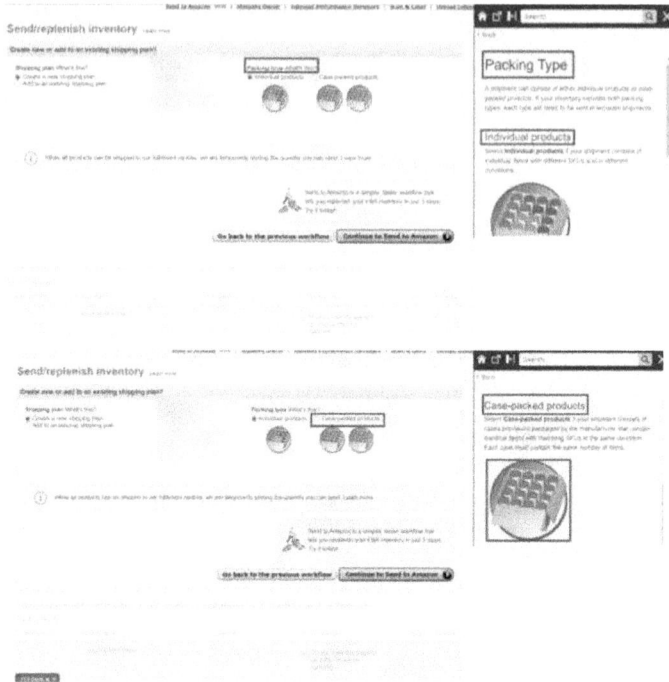

Choose individual products if your shipment contains individual items with different SKUs and in different conditions.

If your products are all the same size, then choose "Case-Packed Products". Basically, this step is for identical items.

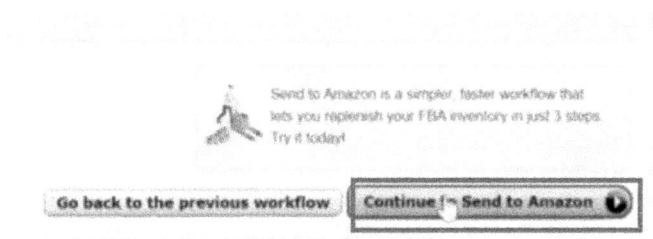

Now scroll down and click "continue to send to Amazon".

Then, on the next screen, fill in "Unit per Case," then "Number of Cases," and click to go to the next page.

Next is "Prep Activities". Here you can choose your product category. Usually, it is "No Prep Needed."

In the next step, Amazon is going to give you the labels. If you have a printer, just click on "Print labels for this page". You'll download this label and send it to your manufacturer for them to put on the boxes containing your product.

In the next step, Amazon will give you the address of their warehouse.

Then click "next." At this stage, Amazon will review all your information.

Next, choose "How will this shipment be packed".

Next, enter your box weight.

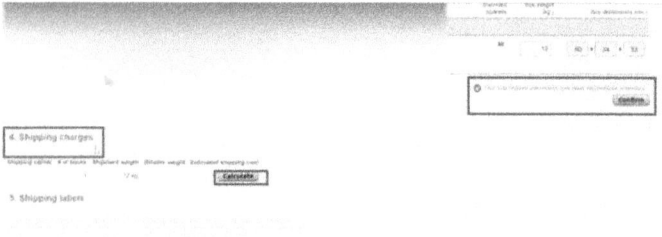

Then Amazon will calculate the shipping charges.

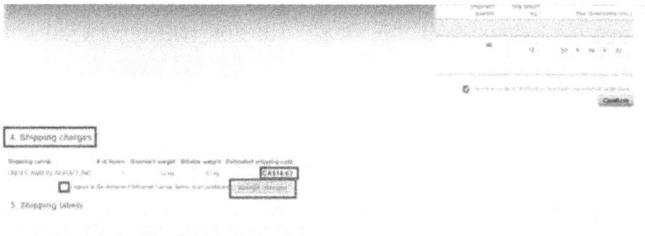

And now you can see the shipping charges.

Tick "I agree to the Amazon Partnered Center Terms and Conditions."

7 rules for Alibaba's success

1.   Always get samples first.

2.   Only orders from Chinese companies

3.   Buy from verified suppliers with more than 5 years of experience.

4.   Use Alibaba's trade assurance.

5.   Use your credit card for purchases under $1000.

6.   For larger payments, use wire transfer. Make sure the beneficiary's name matches the company name.

7.   Always start small and increase your order as you gain experience.

More tips for Alibaba's success!

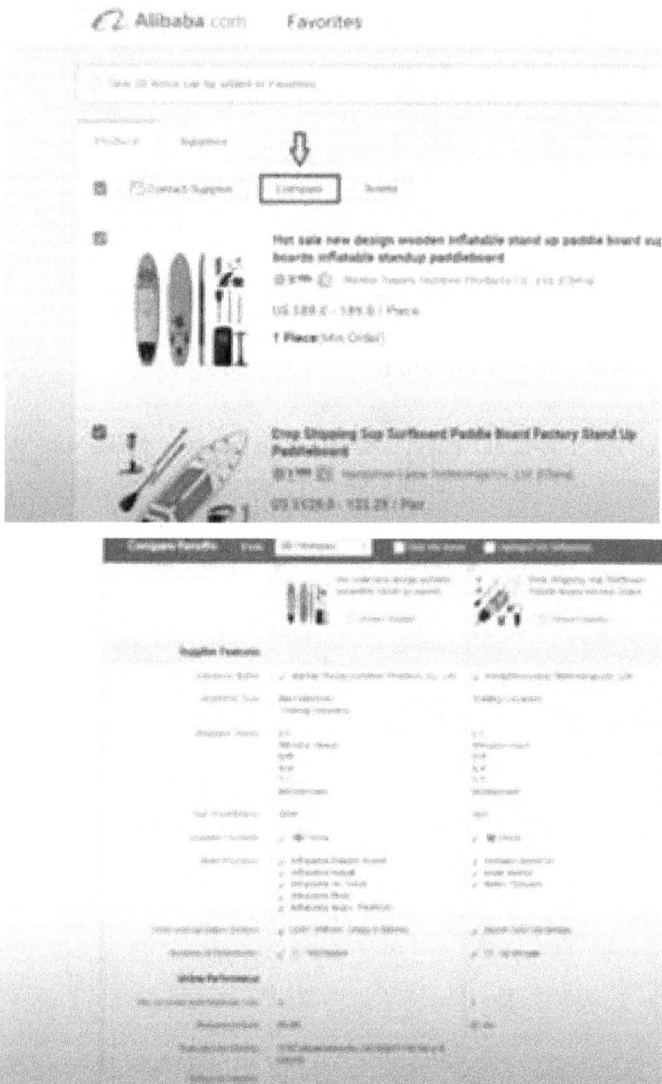

Use the compare feature of Alibaba. This is a useful feature.

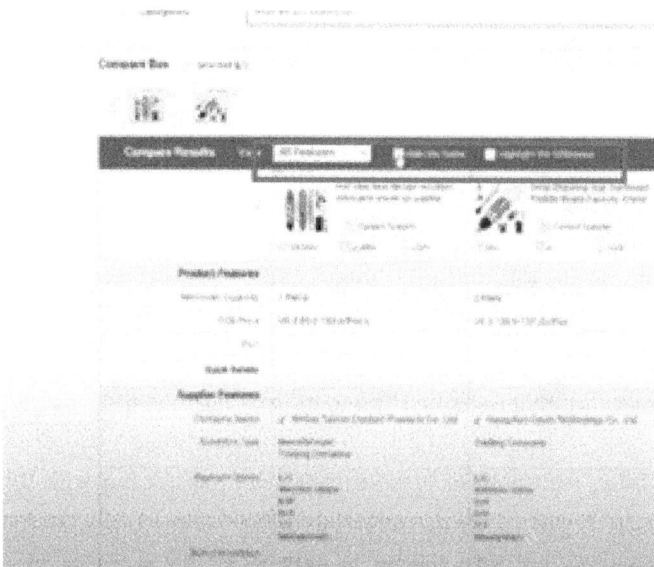

Use the same feature to hide it or highlight the difference. Also, at the bottom of the page, there is an option with which you can contact suppliers. This will save you time.

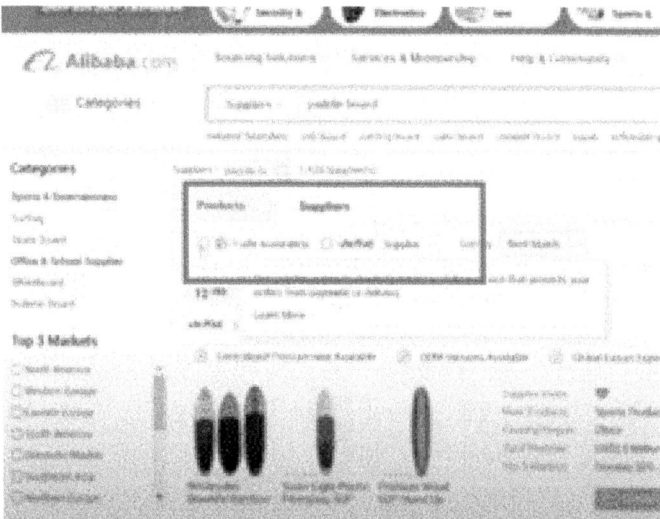

Why source from Verified Suppliers* ?

World-class inspection

Detailed and free inspection report downloads

Verified videos available

Professional suppliers within the industry

When searching for suppliers, check "Trade Assurance" and "Verified". Trade Assurance means that Alibaba protects your payment and allows you to request a refund if your product is unsatisfactory 30 days after delivery. Verified means that the manufacturing is verified by a third-party inspection company.

Lastly, remember to make sure you are contracting with real factories and not trading companies. Real factories only produce one type of product and have a vast knowledge of that product. So they will be able to help you more. On the other hand, trading companies sell a variety of products and do not specialize in any particular product.

Chapter Five

Building Your A+ Listing

Conversion Rate Optimization on Amazon

The product you're selling on Amazon is one that you're passionate about, and it appears to be one that your customers enjoy as well. It's just that you're not seeing the sales figures you'd like to see. In an attempt to have your product seen by the right people, you're spending money on advertising, but nothing seems to be working. What's going on? The root of the problem is your Amazon conversion rate.

One of the most critical indicators of a brand's long-term success on Amazon is its Amazon conversion rate. Even if your goods are the best in the industry, if your conversion rate is low, that product's sales potential will be reduced. With a higher conversion rate and a lower return on investment, higher ranks organically generate more income and put more money in your pocket (ROI). The key to changing the needle lies in examining your conversion rate in greater depth.

What percentage of your Amazon sales are actual sales?

Your Amazon ad's conversion rate is the percentage of clicks that lead to sales. It's a measure of how many individuals click through to your product page and then complete their purchase. That number might assist you in identifying any problems that may be preventing you from selling more.

Is there a way to calculate your Amazon conversion rate?

Calculating your Amazon conversion rate is a matter of a few easy math equations. The formula for calculating it is as follows:

The conversion rate for your merchandise may be found

Conversion Rate = Orders ÷ Page Views (or Sessions)

in your Seller Central Business Reports by clicking on "Detail Page Sales and Traffic by Parent Item." This provides you with accessibility to your product's sales and usage.

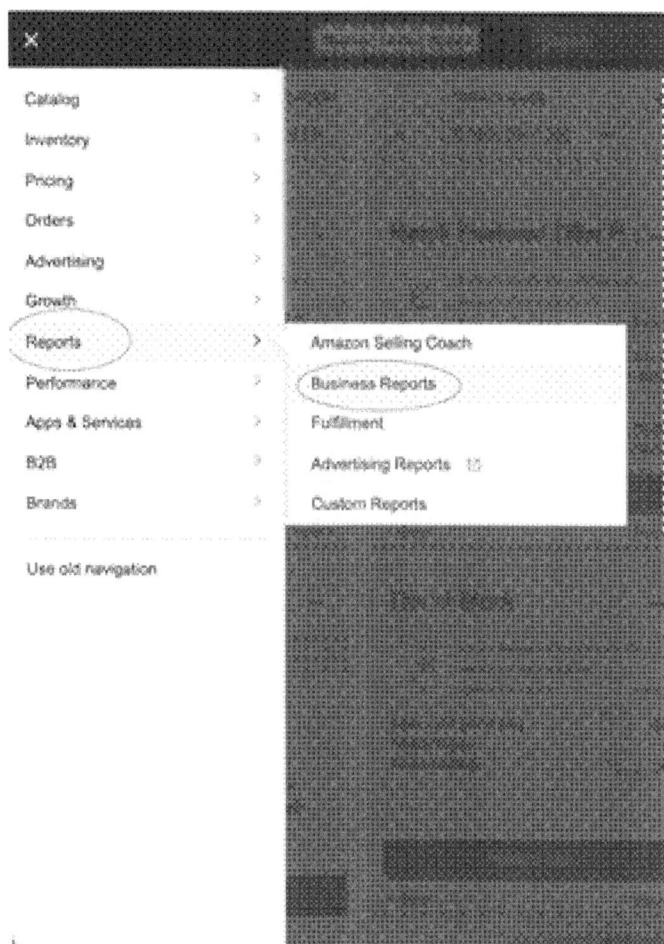

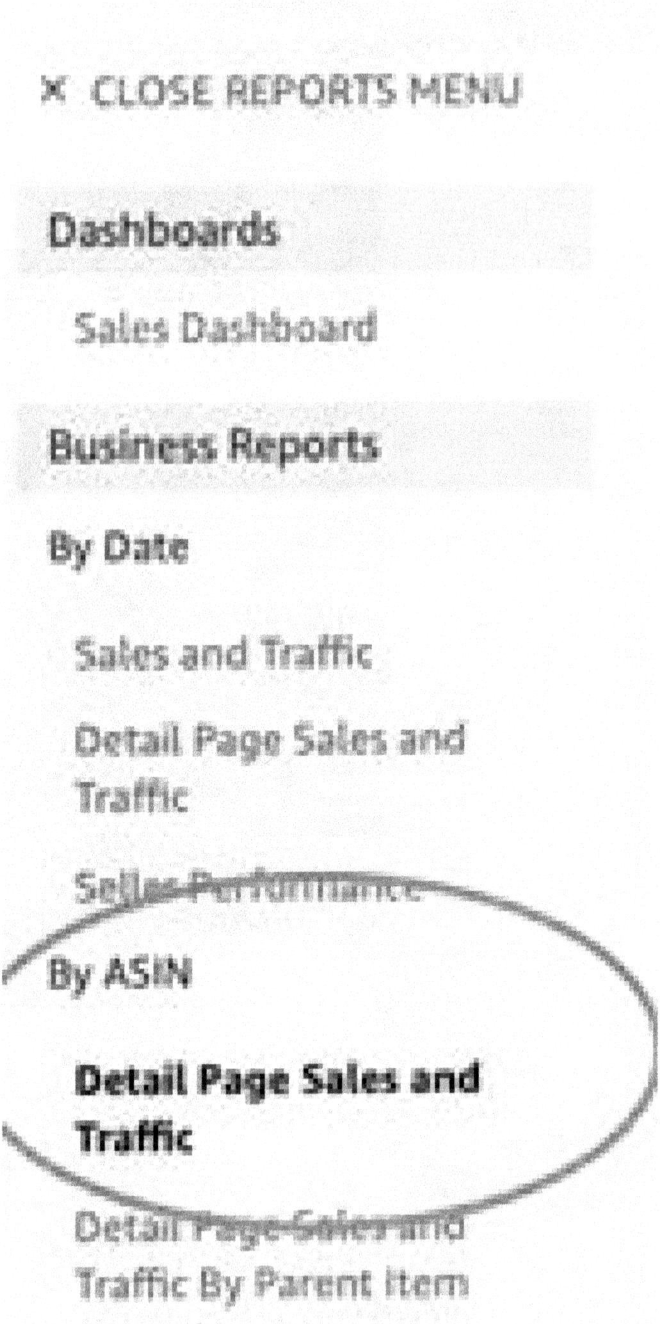

✕ CLOSE REPORTS MENU

Dashboards

Sales Dashboard

Business Reports

By Date

Sales and Traffic

Detail Page Sales and
Traffic

Seller Performance

By ASIN

**Detail Page Sales and
Traffic**

Detail Page Sales and
Traffic By Parent Item

Detail Page Sales and
Traffic By Child Item

Brand Performance

Other

Sales and Orders by
Month

You can select a date range and navigate down the table until you see "Sessions," "Units Ordered," and "Unit Session Percent" on this page.

Business Reports | Detail Page Sales and Traffic Learn more

Sessions	Session Percentage	Page Views	Page Views Percentage	Featured Offer (Buy Box) Percentage	Units Ordered	Units Ordered - B2B	Unit Session Percentage
2,534	0.07%	3,265	0.02%	87.66%	1,601	25	63.18%
1,773	0.05%	2,255	0.05%	85.1%	1,788	25	100.85%
2,503	0.07%	2,924	0.07%	87.76%	1,615	16	64.52%
1,713	0.05%	2,095	0.05%	98.38%	1,777	21	105.74%
2,699	0.08%	3,376	0.08%	94.08%	1,619	22	59.99%
2,425	0.07%	3,101	0.07%	92.81%	1,656	31	68.29%
20,220	0.57%	24,763	0.56%	83.69%	1,597	27	7.9%

"Session count" is the number of unique visitors to your site. Within 24 hours, the very same page will count as a single session regardless of how many times a user accesses it. To get the unit session percent, take your units ordered and divide them by the number of sessions to get your unit session percentage or conversion rate.

What is a reasonable Amazon conversion rate?

If you've discovered how to measure your conversion rate, is it good or bad? Comparing it to Amazon's figures is the most effective method. Among online marketplaces, Amazon has some of the highest conversion rates. This is the reason why many brands choose to sell there. A respectable Amazon conversion rate for non-Prime customers is between 10% and 15%. Because of that, that number drops to 3.32 percent among the top 500 companies because of the frequency with which they are seen. Amazon Prime members have an even higher conversion rate, at 74%. It's vital to keep in mind that a high conversion rate varies depending on the product and the market.

Consumers are likely to shop around and evaluate comparable models before finalizing their buy on Amazon if the product is more costly ($100+). The size of the sample has a significant impact on a high conversion rate. Even if your conversion rate is 50% and you get 10 sales out of every 20 hits, your profit isn't going to be spectacular because you've only made 10 sales. In other words, your conversion rate could look lower at 20% because you only got 100 views with 20 conversions, but in actuality, you got twice as many purchases.

What's the reason for the low conversion?

A lower-than-average conversion rate indicates that either your listing or ad campaign needs improvement, and there are a number of underlying aspects you can explore.

Listing optimization

Product listings that are either uninspiring or ambiguous are often to blame for a decrease in conversion rates. Customer confidence in their ability to understand what you're selling may be at risk because of a poor-quality image or an image stack that just includes one or two images. It's possible that your headline or product description isn't descriptive enough or doesn't contain enough information. If a buyer isn't sure what they're getting from your product when they arrive at your page, they're more likely to shop elsewhere. On the other hand, perhaps your product description is confusing and difficult to follow. To gain clients' trust, an item's description must be simple to understand and informative enough to convince them to make a purchase. Your conversion rate could be dramatically improved if you took the time to fine-tune your ad.

Reviews

Bad or limited reviews are another explanation of low conversion rates. You risk scaring away potential buyers if you have only three stars on a product or negative feedback that has gone unanswered on your listing.

Price

You may also want to think about the cost. You're less likely to earn a sale if your product is overpriced or underpriced. Prices that are too high or too low will drive away clients, so be careful not to overcharge or undercharge. To make sales, you need to keep up with the competition.

Advertising

Listings are one place where you may be losing conversions. Another example is advertising campaigns. You could be spending it on the incorrect keywords or ones that are way too broad. Here's a case in point: Someone is on the search for a "frying pan." This is the Amazon keyword. While selling frying pans, don't mislead customers by calling them "egg pans." You can go one step farther with this. This is a good keyword, but it may not be enough to get to the top of the search results. Why? It covers a wide range. Customers are likely looking for more than simply a frying pan.

They may desire a pan with a lid, a nonstick surface, or even one made of cast iron. Amazon's algorithm is aware of this. When you enter a keyword into the search bar, a list of related words and phrases appears. Like Google Autocomplete, Amazon's suggestions are based on previous customer searches. Nonstick frying pans are the first expected suggestion when someone searches for a "frying pan." This is due to the fact that non-stick pans are frequently requested by other clients.

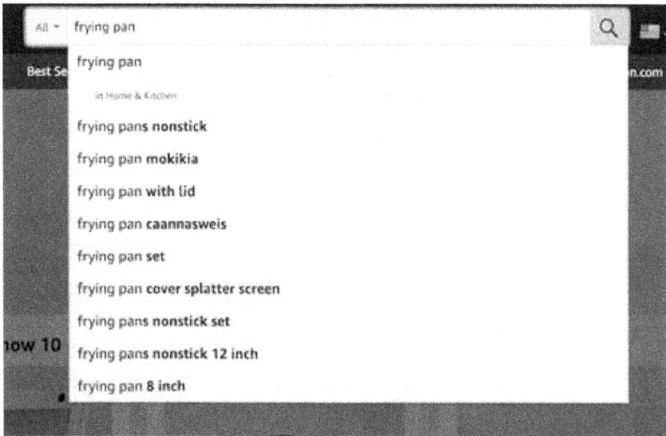

Well, what do you know? A new keyword has been discovered for you. When it comes to targeting your target audience, the more Amazon keywords you utilize (within reason), the better. Additionally, you'll spend heavily on marketing that could be spent on more profitable keywords.

How can you boost your conversion rate on Amazon?

Conversion rate optimization benefits every aspect of your organization, both indirect and direct. A high conversion rate indicates not only that you are making sales, but it also indicates that your goods are liked, and Amazon algorithms will reward your brand by elevating your listing in search rankings, resulting in even more sales. To boost your conversion rate, you want to concentrate on making the customer experience as simple and straightforward as possible for Amazon customers with a high propensity to buy. The following are a few methods for accomplishing this.

o   Optimize your listings: Your listing's visual appeal has a direct bearing on its conversion rate. It's critical to get the main picture, title, and cost of the product faultless because customers scan product listings based on these three elements first. In addition, your picture stacks are critical, particularly as more buyers turn to mobile shopping. There is no listing description or A+ material to be found when visitors click on a mobile device's buy box after clicking on the listing's image stack. Because this may be the first thing customers see, you'll want to make absolutely sure that you have a smart picture stack with good quality photographs as well as instructive photos that can help a consumer understand how to use your product.

The higher your conversion rate, the quicker a customer knows exactly what they're getting. Rather than merely depicting the item, your photos should help you sell it. Incorporate client testimonials, product demonstrations, and answers to frequently asked questions into your photos. If a snapshot of your product in action shows that it alleviates a customer's pain points, you want your potential customers to see that. However, the fact that the image stacks appear first on mobile doesn't mean that you can disregard the associated text. Customers using mobile devices will have to scroll to see the description, but those on desktop computers will see it immediately. You'll want to make sure that the content in the description is simple and easy to skim. Use bullet points to expand on the information included in the picture stacks. By reading your copy, customers should be able to quickly get a feel of who you are as a brand and what your goods can accomplish for them.

o   Bid on specific keywords: Keep in mind that your goal isn't to get the interest of every single Amazon buyer. It's possible that not all of Amazon's users are looking for your product. Shoppers that understand precisely what they want and are ready to acquire it are your target audience. As a result, bidding on specific and unique keywords might help your brand reach these consumers more efficiently and quickly.

o   Offer discounts: If people know they'll be receiving a good price on a product, they're more likely to buy it. Discounts are obviously not a good idea all the time, but they can be an excellent method to enhance your conversion rate. It ensures that your products remain visible and competitive.

o   Using reviews (or "social proof") is a good strategy: Unless there's enough social proof to persuade a buyer to buy a product, they won't do so when they see it for sale. Incorporating positive customer feedback into your copy is one method to achieve this, as is responding promptly to negative feedback. This will allay the fears of potential customers and provide them with the assurance that they're going to have a positive experience. You can also use Amazon's product badges to boost your credibility: Amazon's Choice, Best Seller, and Climate Pledge Friendly are just a few examples.

o   Create a sales funnel that works across all channels: To boost your conversion rates, you can use a landing page to funnel sales from other platforms, such as Instagram or Facebook, to your Amazon listing. This gives clients the opportunity to learn more about your products before they decide to buy them from your website. The likelihood of them converting is great if they like what they see on your landing page and go to your product listing. It takes a little more work, but it's a method for attracting consumers who have a high level of focus.

o   Enhance the experience of your clients: Conversion rates are more likely to be higher for brands that go above and beyond to make the purchasing experience pleasant for their customers. Customers who are loyal are more likely to buy from a company that instills trust and enthusiasm in their brand, resulting in increased sales.

Conversion Rate Optimization on Amazon

The product you're selling on Amazon is one that you're passionate about, and it appears to be one that your customers enjoy as well. It's just that you're not seeing the sales figures you'd like to see. In an attempt to have your product seen by the right people, you're spending money on advertising, but nothing seems to be working. What's going on? The root of the problem is your Amazon conversion rate.

One of the most critical indicators of a brand's long-term success on Amazon is its Amazon conversion rate. Even if your goods are the best in the industry, if your conversion rate is low, that product's sales potential will be reduced. With a higher conversion rate and a lower return on investment, higher ranks organically generate more income and put more money in your pocket (ROI). The key to changing the needle lies in examining your conversion rate in greater depth.

What percentage of your Amazon sales are actual sales?

Your Amazon ad's conversion rate is the percentage of clicks that lead to sales. It's a measure of how many individuals click through to your product page and then complete their purchase. That number might assist you in identifying any problems that may be preventing you from selling more.

Is there a way to calculate your Amazon conversion rate?

Calculating your Amazon conversion rate is a matter of a few easy math equations. The formula for calculating it is as follows:

The conversion rate for your merchandise may be found

Conversion Rate = Orders ÷ Page Views (or Sessions)

in your Seller Central Business Reports by clicking on "Detail Page Sales and Traffic by Parent Item." This provides you with accessibility to your product's sales and usage.

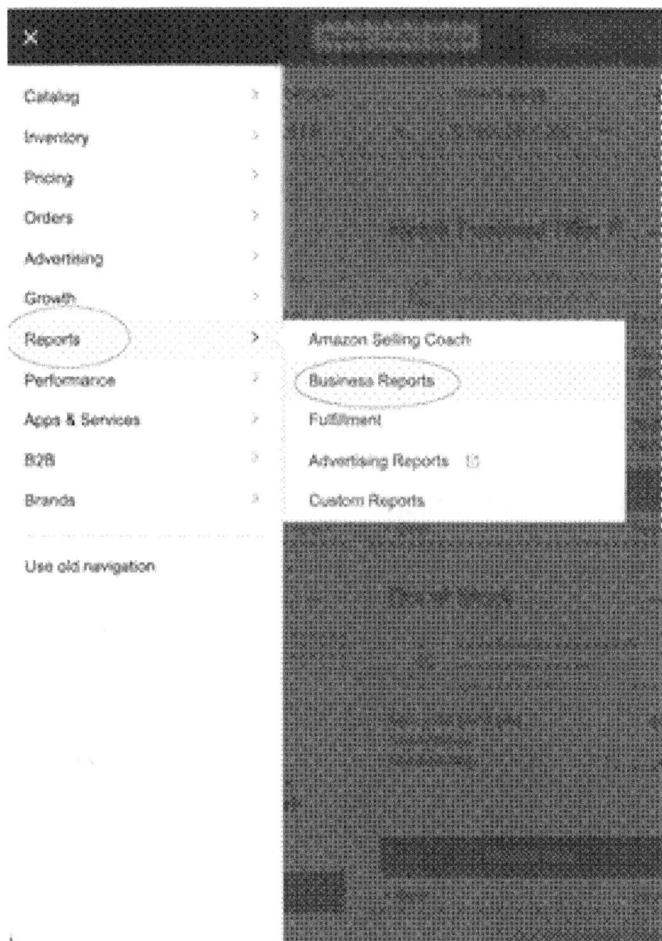

✕ CLOSE REPORTS MENU

Dashboards

Sales Dashboard

Business Reports

By Date

Sales and Traffic

Detail Page Sales and
Traffic

Seller Performance

By ASIN

**Detail Page Sales and
Traffic**

Detail Page Sales and
Traffic By Parent Item

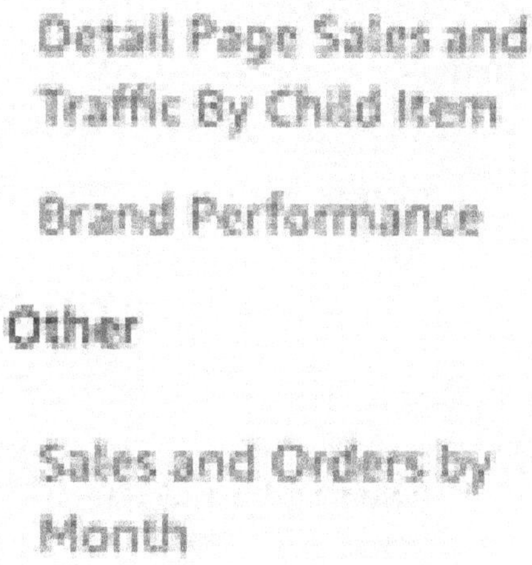

Detail Page Sales and
Traffic By Child Item

Brand Performance

Other

Sales and Orders by
Month

You can select a date range and navigate down the table until you see "Sessions," "Units Ordered," and "Unit Session Percent" on this page.

Business Reports | Detail Page Sales and Traffic Learn more

Sessions	Session Percentage	Page Views	Page Views Percentage	Featured Offer (Buy Box) Percentage	Units Ordered	Units Ordered - B2B	Unit Session Percentage
2,554	0.07%	5,265	0.07%	87.66%	1,601	25	63.18%
1,775	0.05%	2,255	0.05%	85.1%	1,788	25	100.95%
2,503	0.07%	2,924	0.07%	87.76%	1,615	16	64.52%
1,713	0.05%	2,095	0.05%	98.38%	1,777	21	103.74%
2,699	0.08%	3,376	0.08%	94.08%	1,619	22	59.99%
2,425	0.07%	3,101	0.07%	92.81%	1,656	51	68.29%
20,220	0.57%	24,763	0.56%	85.69%	1,597	27	7.9%

"Session count" is the number of unique visitors to your site. Within 24 hours, the very same page will count as a single session regardless of how many times a user accesses it. To get the unit session percent, take your units ordered and divide them by the number of sessions to get your unit session percentage or conversion rate.

What is a reasonable Amazon conversion rate?

If you've discovered how to measure your conversion rate, is it good or bad? Comparing it to Amazon's figures is the most effective method. Among online marketplaces, Amazon has some of the highest conversion rates. This is the reason why many brands choose to sell there. A respectable Amazon conversion rate for non-Prime customers is between 10% and 15%. Because of that, that number drops to 3.32 percent among the top 500 companies because of the frequency with which they are seen. Amazon Prime members have an even higher conversion rate, at 74%. It's vital to keep in mind that a high conversion rate varies depending on the product and the market.

Consumers are likely to shop around and evaluate comparable models before finalizing their buy on Amazon if the product is more costly ($100+). The size of the sample has a significant impact on a high conversion rate. Even if your conversion rate is 50% and you get 10 sales out of every 20 hits, your profit isn't going to be spectacular because you've only made 10 sales. In other words, your conversion rate could look lower at 20% because you only got 100 views with 20 conversions, but in actuality, you got twice as many purchases.

What's the reason for the low conversion?

A lower-than-average conversion rate indicates that either your listing or ad campaign needs improvement, and there are a number of underlying aspects you can explore.

Listing optimization

Product listings that are either uninspiring or ambiguous are often to blame for a decrease in conversion rates. Customer confidence in their ability to understand what you're selling may be at risk because of a poor-quality image or an image stack that just includes one or two images. It's possible that your headline or product description isn't descriptive enough or doesn't contain enough information. If a buyer isn't sure what they're getting from your product when they arrive at your page, they're more likely to shop elsewhere. On the other hand, perhaps your product description is confusing and difficult to follow. To gain clients' trust, an item's description must be simple to understand and informative enough to convince them to make a purchase. Your conversion rate could be dramatically improved if you took the time to fine-tune your ad.

Reviews

Bad or limited reviews are another explanation of low conversion rates. You risk scaring away potential buyers if you have only three stars on a product or negative feedback that has gone unanswered on your listing.

Price

You may also want to think about the cost. You're less likely to earn a sale if your product is overpriced or underpriced. Prices that are too high or too low will drive away clients, so be careful not to overcharge or undercharge. To make sales, you need to keep up with the competition.

Advertising

Listings are one place where you may be losing conversions. Another example is advertising campaigns. You could be spending it on the incorrect keywords or ones that are way too broad. Here's a case in point: Someone is on the search for a "frying pan." This is the Amazon keyword. While selling frying pans, don't mislead customers by calling them "egg pans." You can go one step farther with this. This is a good keyword, but it may not be enough to get to the top of the search results. Why? It covers a wide range. Customers are likely looking for more than simply a frying pan.

They may desire a pan with a lid, a nonstick surface, or even one made of cast iron. Amazon's algorithm is aware of this. When you enter a keyword into the search bar, a list of related words and phrases appears. Like Google Autocomplete, Amazon's suggestions are based on previous customer searches. Nonstick frying pans are the first expected suggestion when someone searches for a "frying pan." This is due to the fact that non-stick pans are frequently requested by other clients.

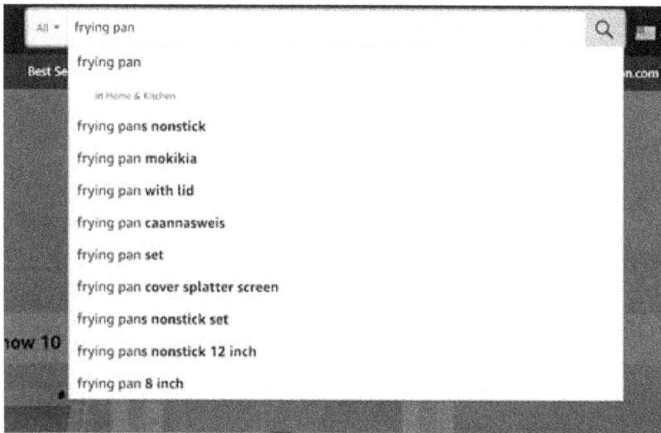

Well, what do you know? A new keyword has been discovered for you. When it comes to targeting your target audience, the more Amazon keywords you utilize (within reason), the better. Additionally, you'll spend heavily on marketing that could be spent on more profitable keywords.

How can you boost your conversion rate on Amazon?

Conversion rate optimization benefits every aspect of your organization, both indirect and direct. A high conversion rate indicates not only that you are making sales, but it also indicates that your goods are liked, and Amazon algorithms will reward your brand by elevating your listing in search rankings, resulting in even more sales. To boost your conversion rate, you want to concentrate on making the customer experience as simple and straightforward as possible for Amazon customers with a high propensity to buy. The following are a few methods for accomplishing this.

o   Optimize your listings: Your listing's visual appeal has a direct bearing on its conversion rate. It's critical to get the main picture, title, and cost of the product faultless because customers scan product listings based on these three elements first. In addition, your picture stacks are critical, particularly as more buyers turn to mobile shopping. There is no listing description or A+ material to be found when visitors click on a mobile device's buy box after clicking on the listing's image stack. Because this may be the first thing customers see, you'll want to make absolutely sure that you have a smart picture stack with good quality photographs as well as instructive photos that can help a consumer understand how to use your product.

The higher your conversion rate, the quicker a customer knows exactly what they're getting. Rather than merely depicting the item, your photos should help you sell it. Incorporate client testimonials, product demonstrations, and answers to frequently asked questions into your photos. If a snapshot of your product in action shows that it alleviates a customer's pain points, you want your potential customers to see that. However, the fact that the image stacks appear first on mobile doesn't mean that you can disregard the associated text. Customers using mobile devices will have to scroll to see the description, but those on desktop computers will see it immediately. You'll want to make sure that the content in the description is simple and easy to skim. Use bullet points to expand on the information included in the picture stacks. By reading your copy, customers should be able to quickly get a feel of who you are as a brand and what your goods can accomplish for them.

o   Bid on specific keywords: Keep in mind that your goal isn't to get the interest of every single Amazon buyer. It's possible that not all of Amazon's users are looking for your product. Shoppers that understand precisely what they want and are ready to acquire it are your target audience. As a result, bidding on specific and unique keywords might help your brand reach these consumers more efficiently and quickly.

o   Offer discounts: If people know they'll be receiving a good price on a product, they're more likely to buy it. Discounts are obviously not a good idea all the time, but they can be an excellent method to enhance your conversion rate. It ensures that your products remain visible and competitive.

o   Using reviews (or "social proof") is a good strategy: Unless there's enough social proof to persuade a buyer to buy a product, they won't do so when they see it for sale. Incorporating positive customer feedback into your copy is one method to achieve this, as is responding promptly to negative feedback. This will allay the fears of potential customers and provide them with the assurance that they're going to have a positive experience. You can also use Amazon's product badges to boost your credibility: Amazon's Choice, Best Seller, and Climate Pledge Friendly are just a few examples.

o   Create a sales funnel that works across all channels: To boost your conversion rates, you can use a landing page to funnel sales from other platforms, such as Instagram or Facebook, to your Amazon listing. This gives clients the opportunity to learn more about your products before they decide to buy them from your website. The likelihood of them converting is great if they like what they see on your landing page and go to your product listing. It takes a little more work, but it's a method for attracting consumers who have a high level of focus.

o   Enhance the experience of your clients: Conversion rates are more likely to be higher for brands that go above and beyond to make the purchasing experience pleasant for their customers. Customers who are loyal are more likely to buy from a company that instills trust and enthusiasm in their brand, resulting in increased sales.

Optimizing Your Amazon Product Listings for Increased Sales in 2022

Whether you're just starting out selling on Amazon or already have a successful bestseller, these pointers will help you succeed at every stage of the process. By checking out these primary pillars below, you will get a sense of what goes into developing an Amazon product listing that is loved and cared for by Amazon's algorithm.

Your product listing on Amazon should focus on the following six areas in order to rise to the top of the page:

Six Fundamental Elements of Amazon Product Listing Optimization

1.   Product Title

2.   Product Features

3.   Product Description

4.   Product Images

5.   Backend keywords

6.   Customer reviews

As a starting point, familiarize yourself with the Amazon search engine.

Is There a Formula for Amazon to Use When Ranking Your Product?

In the same way that Google evaluates search queries for various keywords, Amazon's algorithms seek to serve the most relevant and high-performing listings to users. It uses a variety of ranking elements, both direct and indirect, to assign each product a score. Sales velocity, pricing, stock availability, delivery method, reviews, photos, A+ content, and keyword relevance for product titles, attributes, descriptions, and backend search phrases are just a few of the considerations that need to be taken into consideration. The entries with the highest scores are given the most prominent spots in the search results.

What Is Amazon's Ranking Algorithm Based On?

Product listings are evaluated by Amazon using the A10 algorithm to see whether they are relevant and trustworthy. Amazon's main algorithm is in charge of ensuring that customers only receive the highest-quality goods for their hard-earned cash.

On Amazon, what does one mean by "Listing Optimization?"

On Amazon, listing optimization is the process of upgrading your product pages to make them more likely to appear in the Amazon search results for specific keywords. For your product, this leads to more hits, leads, and sales. Finding new keywords, enhancing your product photos, and gaining more consumer feedback are all part of the process. As personal suggestions and a way to boost Amazon's social proof, these reviews are a big benefit.

What are Amazon's keywords?

Consumers use Amazon keywords (also known as search phrases or queries) to locate and purchase products on the online retailer's site. keywords might be as broad as "Coffee mugs" or as narrowly defined as "hardened steel coffee mugs with handles and lids," depending on your needs. You may make it easier for Amazon to comprehend your product's purpose by including relevant keywords in your listing.

This brings up an essential point:

Where Can I Find Amazon Keywords?

Various third-party keyword research tools can help you discover Amazon keywords. Direct keyword extraction from Amazon's Brand Analytics database is made possible by these tools. These crawlers can also sift through competitor listings to see what keywords they are employing.

When looking for keywords for your product, don't forget to make use of the Amazon keyword suggestion tool as well. When you use Amazon's search bar to enter your niche's core keyword, Amazon will have auto suggestions that you can use to enhance your keywords. This is a great way to niche down and get very specific with your keywords. Remember that the more specific and relevant your keywords the higher your conversion rates will be and increasing conversion rates is the best way to achieve and maximize profits.

How Do I Choose Amazon Listing Keywords?

Your Amazon listing should include high-and medium-volume traffic keywords related to your products. Both short-tail and long-tail keywords can be found here. Instead of relying heavily on the first group of keywords, your approach should be to employ the second set sparingly.

Why? Short-tail keywords are broad in nature because they're so short. They're also incredibly competitive, and they don't convert very well. When it comes to long-tail keywords, the opposite is true. There's a good chance they'll generate a lot of hits. It's also easier to rank for them because there isn't as much competition. Interestingly, Amazon boosts your short-tail keyword rankings when it sees your goods appearing for long-tail keywords. We call this phenomenon the "halo effect." Long-tail and short-tail keywords with high search volumes and relevance to your product are recommended when optimizing your Amazon product listing.

How Can I Make My Amazon Product Listing More Profitable?

Amazon product listings can be improved using these six steps:

1.   Step 1: The most important information about your product should be included in a keyword-focused title.

2.   Step 2: Use bullet points to illustrate why people should buy your product. Avoid the recurrence of long-tail keywords.

3.   Step 3: By upgrading your current one, you can create an intriguing product description. The first 200 characters of your product description should convey the product's worth by emphasizing its use and applicability.

4.   Step 4: Complete the keyword fields on the backend.

5.   Step 5: Keep Amazon's requirements in mind while using photography services to create product visuals. At least six photos are required.

6.   Step 6: Gather customer feedback. However, ensure that the reviews are genuine, or else Amazon may ban your listing (or worse).

Keep in mind that optimizing your Amazon listings for mobile should be a part of your overall strategy. Let's take a closer look at each of the optimization phases one by one:

1.   Amazon SEO. Optimize the title of your Amazon product with reference to the primary keyword. In Amazon listings, your product title is the part that gets the most clicks, making it the most critical part of your listing. Imagine yourself in a bookstore. What draws you to picking up a book off the shelf and perusing the offerings? You're right. It's the title or the cover. It's exactly the same situation here. Customers who have never heard of your brand will be drawn to your product page if your product listing title catches their eye. Make the most of it by enhancing it.

·   Include the name of your company.

·   Enter the core keyword you want to target

·   Product specifications, such as height, color, number, and model, should be included.

·   Ensure that your customers have the information necessary to make an informed purchase decision when they search for your goods.

Product Title Guidelines: What to Do and What Not to Do

·   The first letter of each word should be capitalized.

·   Don't use abbreviations when referring to measurements (i.e., pounds, inches, tablets, etc.).

·   Make sure the numbers are displayed in numerical form.

·   Don't mention the price or the seller's information.

·   Use lowercase letters and numbers instead of all-caps.

·   Don't utilize commercials (i.e., sales, bestsellers, discounts, etc.).

·   Avoid using symbols (such as $, &, or ®) in your writing.

How Many Words Can an Amazon Title Feature?

Amazon's product titles can be anything from 80 to 200 characters long, based on the item's category and subcategory. Keep it to a maximum of 130 characters if at all possible.

Creating Mobile-Friendly Titles for Your Listings

An item's title can only be shown for the first 80 characters on mobile devices. For the best results, use your core keyword at the top of the page, perhaps even just after your brand name. Using the formula outlined below, you may create an interesting product title:

Bad Example

Let's start with a dreadful product name. The item title in the image below is not detailed enough to be rated highly on Amazon. The CTR (Click-Through-Rate) of the ad will be impacted as well.

Lux Long Ring 60 minute Classic Timer
by Lux
$11⁵⁵ prime
FREE Shipping on eligible orders

More Buying Choices
$5.40 (19 new offers)

★★★★☆ · 118
Product Description
... Lux's Iconic Short Ring Timers Are The Most Recognized And Best Selling ...

Good Example

The following is an example of a well-optimized ad. Since this Habor digital kitchen timer offers a great deal of information in its product title, it ranks highly on Amazon.

Habor Digital Kitchen Timer Clock Cooking Timer Multifunction with Big Digits, Loud Alarm, Magnetic Backing Stand, and Memory for Cooking Baking Exercise-Blue/White
by Habor
$7⁹⁹ $21.05 prime
FREE Shipping on eligible orders

★★★★☆ · 262
10% off each with purchase of 1 items See Details
Product Features
... Would ensures you can hear this kitchen timer's alarm in another room...

2.   Optimize Your Listings by Creating Bullet Points That Appeal to Your Customers. A product's Amazon ranking is greatly aided by using bullet points in its description. Unless you're a member of Amazon Vendors, you're limited to five bullet points in your product description. To avoid having your listing read like a maze of meaningless gibberish, keep your text to a bare minimum.

·   Focus on the advantages of your product rather than the disadvantages.

·   Create content that persuades potential buyers that your items can solve their problems.

·   Each bullet point should contain at least one long-tail keyword.

What is the maximum length of Amazon bullet points?

It's best to limit the length of each bullet point to less than 200 characters for better conversion rates. A10 simply indexes and ranks your bullet points' first 1000 characters.

Creating Mobile-Friendly Listing Bullet Points

Customers using mobile devices can only see about 400 characters of Amazon's bullet points, making it more difficult to persuade them to buy your product.

Bad Example

Consider the following product listing, which makes use of just three bullet points: It's critical to maximize the use of your goods.

Suncast Elevated Feeding Tray, Large
★★★★☆ ·   833 customer reviews | 52 answered questions

6'   ۹   Get the Best Deal
Price: $21.99

In Stock.
This item ships to Taiwan, Republic of China. Want it Monday, Oct. 23? Order within 22 hrs 53 mins and choose AmazonGlobal Priority Shipping at checkout. Learn more
Ships from and sold by Amazon.com. Gift-wrap available.

Size: Large

· Feeding tray can be used on floor or add legs for additional height
· Legs store securely under the tray
· Two 3" stainless steel bowls included

Compare with similar items

Used & new (17) from $17.59 & FREE shipping on orders over $25.00. Details

Good Example

A targeted Amazon listing, on the other hand, uses appealing bullet points and all-caps language to drive home the argument. They have a constant tone and describe the product's advantages and features very well.

3.   Keep the product information content focused on Amazon SEO. There is a lot of room in the product description to incorporate more information that will entice customers to buy. Use this opportunity to properly communicate your brand's value and provide a thorough explanation of your product's functionality.

·   Be concise.

·   Separate the content into short paragraphs to make it easier to read.

·   Integrate keywords that aren't in the title or bullet points into your content.

·   Don't over-promise, deceive, or misrepresent.

·   Talk about real-world examples.

·   Introduce the concept of scarcity into your writing (wherever possible).

How Many Words Can You Use in an Amazon Product Description?

Amazon product descriptions have a character limit of 2000 characters. Your audience is going to need a lot more than that to comprehend your argument.

Creating a Mobile-Friendly Product Description

The first 200 words of product information are only displayed on mobile devices by Amazon. Taking this into consideration, you should tailor your content appropriately.

Bad Example

This description of an item serves as an excellent illustration of poor copywriting. There isn't a lot of information regarding the product for customers to go on.

Product description

Natural Balance 725433606080 LIT TREAT LIT VENISON & SWEET POTATO 8oz

Good Example

The description of a product should be split into short, digestible pieces. Simply put, it's a great way to get your point through in a way that's both succinct and powerful.

Product description

Size: 180 Count (Pack of 1)

You love your pup!

Lloyd and Lucy's Hip and Joint Supplement packs a powerful punch of superior ingredients.

Why not offer your dog a treat that not only tastes great but is also great for them?

Lots of dogs have given our Hip and Joint Supplement "two-paws" up for its amazing liver taste, so owners have started to offer the supplement as a treat during the day. So use the supplements each morning or night as a special treat!

And there's NO RISK.

If your dog doesn't like the taste, just contact us within 45 days, and we'll GIVE YOU YOUR MONEY BACK! That's how confident we are in our YUMMYLICIOUS formula.

We care about your dog. We really do.

That's why we offer the best ingredients at a great value. We want happy, healthy dogs just as much as you do.

Order today, and see why so many customers have given us 5 star reviews for our product and our customer service.

Is it possible to include HTML in Amazon product details?

Amazon's product information no longer allows HTML tags due to technical limitations. For formatting purposes, line breaks can still be used.

4.   Enhancing Your Listing: Refresh Your Backend Keywords. As a way to make your product easier to find, Amazon gives you the option to edit your listing's backend SEO keywords. For a competitive edge, take advantage of the fact that many vendors keep their backend keywords blank.

What is a backend keyword?

It is possible for Amazon bots to scan and index backend (or hidden) keywords that are not visible to the general public. SEO relies heavily on them, as they help your product get to the top of the search results.

Amazon backend keywords are classified into five categories:

i)   Keywords for Intended Use

ii)   Other characteristics

iii)   Keywords for a Specific Audience

iv)   Subject Matter

v)   Search Terms

What are Amazon's "Intended Use" keywords?

The term "intended use" refers to the activities, circumstances, or locations for which a product is designed. Halloween, baseball, the kitchen, and the holiday season are just a few examples.

Are there any other attributes that are available on Amazon?

These supplementary qualities are used to describe the additional features and characteristics of a product. Additional relevant keywords include rechargeable, antique, weatherproof, etc.

What are Amazon's "Target Audience Keywords"?

The term "target audience" refers to a particular target market for a product. Large dogs, and young children are all good examples.

What is the Amazon listing's subject matter?

Amazon uses subject matter to fully understand your product. A backend keyword is likely the most crucial form of keyword to have. Most product categories give you five subject matter slots, each of which can hold up to 50 characters of data. Subject keywords include children's attention toys, exercise mattresses for on-the-go women, and pressure-sealed carrier bags.

What are some of the most popular Amazon search terms?

Search terms, such as subject matter keywords, help Amazon better understand your goods. These ASINs, or brand names, should be free of rivals' ASINs and unique. In the search terms area, there is a maximum of 250 bytes of characters.

Should Commas Be Used To Separate Backend Keywords From Each Other?

You cannot use a semicolon, a comma, or any other punctuation marks to separate several backend keywords from each other on Amazon's search results page. The best way to separate them is to use single spaces.

5.   Use High-Resolution Product Images to Boost Amazon Search Engine Rankings. Listings are only as good as their product photos. The visual appeal of your product listing has a significant influence on Amazon customers' purchasing decisions. As a result, you can't afford to fall short of their expectations. Experienced Amazon listing optimization service providers who have expertise in product photography are recommended.

·   Your primary image should have a snow-white background.

·   Images with a resolution of no less than 2000 x 2000 pixels perform optimally.

·   The JPEG file format is the most popular.

·   Text should be used sparingly in graphics.

·   Consider using one primary image, one lifestyle image, one-dimension image, one feature image, one instruction image, and one before and after photograph.

·   Add your target term to the file name of the image you're seeking to rank for.

Product photography can take on a variety of styles, including 3D rendering for a more modern appearance. But it can feel a little out of place. However, the final result may not be as seamless as a 3D image when using real-life photography to convey trust and authenticity. Lastly, there's a hybrid model, which combines 3D graphics techniques with real-world images.

You can only have so many images on Amazon.

The maximum number of photographs you can include in your product listing is nine. However, the product description on Amazon only shows seven photographs. If you go to the gallery, you'll find the other two photos.

Creating Mobile-Friendly Listing Images

When it comes to seeing images, a PC and a smartphone can offer vastly different experiences. Portrait images, in our opinion, are ideal for mobile devices. Before completing the optimization of your product listing, make sure to test it on both mobile and desktop devices.

Bad Example

An example of a light-up dog leash seller's primary image is shown here. Just by glancing at the primary image, it's hard to determine what the product is or what it does. In addition, the image violates Amazon's image requirements because it contains a non-white background. That could explain why the listing appears so far down in the list of results.

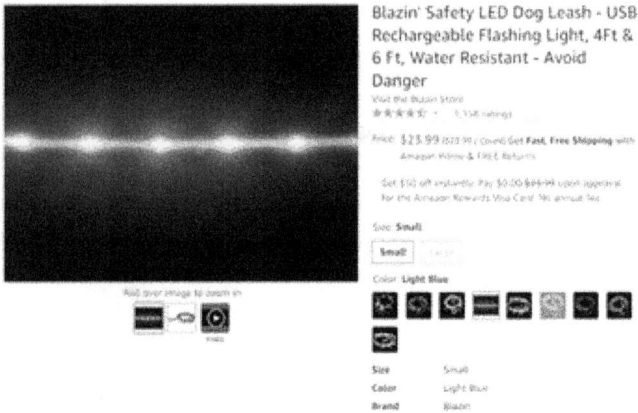

Good Example

This is a great example of how to properly shoot a product. The seller used high-resolution photographs and followed all directions precisely.

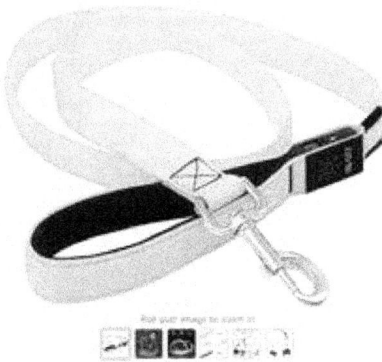

BSEEN LED Lighted Dog
Leash - USB Rechargeable
Nylon Puppy Lead, Safety
Dog Lights for Night Walking
(47 Inch, Neon Green)

6.   Boost Your Product's Ranking Using Listing Optimization. Finally, there are reviews of the products themselves. They're a marketing powerhouse and can help persuade buyers to buy your stuff. You'll see a boost in your product's ranking on Amazon as a result of this. Amazon keeps a careful eye on how you collect reviews because they can have such a significant impact on your listing. You can rest assured that Amazon will punish you if it discovers anything questionable about the method you used to secure customer reviews for your product. It is imperative that you obtain product reviews in a lawful manner!

o   Become a member of Vine

o   Product inserts can be used to encourage people to post reviews of your product.

o   Post-sale, you may use the "Submit Feedback" button in Seller Central to ask for feedback from your consumers.

How to Make Changes to an Existing Amazon Product Listing

The following are the processes of optimizing and editing an old listing:

1.   You must log in to your Seller Central account by clicking here.

2.   Navigate to the Inventory tab and select "Manage Inventory" from the drop-down menu.

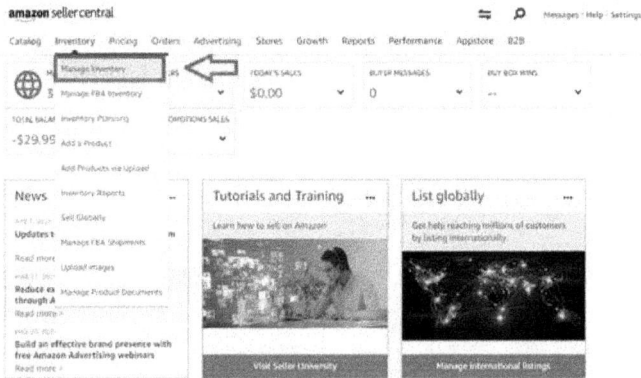

3.   To the right of the listing that needs optimization, click "Edit."

4.   On the subsequent page, click the appropriate tab and make the necessary modifications.

You must wait 24 hours after submitting the modified version in order for the changes to take effect. Feel free to contact the Seller Central support staff and start a "Fix a product page" case with Amazon if the adjustments do not show on the product page after several attempts. This should take care of the situation.

How can I make changes to multiple Amazon product listings at the same time?

By utilizing the flat-file upload function included in Seller Central, you can make bulk edits to Amazon product listings. Those who sell in bulk will benefit the most from this feature since it allows them to make adjustments and add content to their product pages with little effort. Many sellers are apprehensive about making modifications to their existing listings, especially if they are performing well in the market. But keep in mind that the top positions on Amazon must be earned and retained through hard work. Your rival is constantly on the lookout for an opportunity to seize your position. If you don't improve your product listings on a regular basis, they'll catch up with you sooner or later.

Chapter Six

Getting started with Advertising

What is Amazon PPC?

Third-party sellers can use Amazon PPC to construct ad campaigns for their products and increase sales on the online retailer's site. Amazon charges advertisers a fee each time a customer clicks on an ad they've placed (pay-per-click model). As a result, Amazon PPC advertising has grown into a potent marketing tool. By utilizing Amazon's advertising platform, sellers and vendors can "purchase" their way to the top of Amazon's search results page. Every year, the number of vendors taking advantage of Amazon's advertising opportunities grows considerably. If you don't have a clear strategy in place, it may be tough to meet your Amazon PPC objectives.

Amazon PPC Advertising Types

Advertisements on Amazon can be classified as one of three types: sponsored products, sponsored brands, or sponsored display advertisements (PDAs). Sponsored Products are comparable to Google AdWords, which allow you to advertise specific items in Amazon search engine results and on product description pages. These are keyword and ASIN-focused ads.

Among Amazon's advertisements, sponsored products are the most often seen.

As the name implies, "Sponsored Brand" ads allow companies to promote their products with a custom title and logo above Amazon search results (and in other places), and they can direct customers to their Amazon Stores page or a custom landing page on Amazon. Video advertising with links to product information pages is also now available.

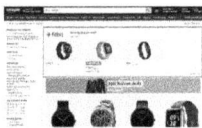

Advertisements that direct customers to Amazon product detail pages are often known as "sponsored display advertising." They use Amazon and other websites to target buyers who have visited or re-visited specific products on Amazon and offer relevant adverts to them.

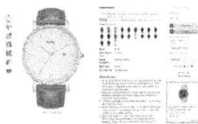

Where can you see Amazon ads?

o   Sponsored Products ads. Promoted product advertising can be found at the top or bottom of Amazon search results, as well as on product description pages as part of an ad rotation.

o   Sponsored Brands ads. Amazon's search results page features sponsored brand advertisements in a variety of locations, including the "top real estate" position directly above the results. It is possible for sponsored brands' advertising to show up on product pages.

o   Sponsored Display ads. Advertisements are displayed on Amazon product pages, adjacent to search results, or on third-party sites and apps according to a specific targeting strategy (product/views targeting).

Who is eligible to advertise on Amazon?

An Amazon advertisement can be used by both vendors and sellers. However, sellers must be registered in the Amazon Brand Directory, as shown in the chart below. Why does it matter whether you're dealing with vendors or sellers? Often referred to as "third-party sellers," Amazon shoppers can purchase things directly from third-party retailers. For first-party vendors, Amazon purchases their products in bulk and then resells them to its consumers. Both FBM (Fulfillment by Merchant) and FBA (Fulfillment by Amazon) products can be advertised on Amazon. Below is a summary of each sort of Amazon ad's eligibility requirements:

ELIGIBILITY CRITERIA	SPONSORED PRODUCTS	SPONSORED BRANDS	SPONSORED DISPLAY
General	Active account in good standing with Amazon		
	The ability to ship to the country in which you're advertising		
	Valid payment method		
Seller Type	Professional seller, vendor, Kindle Direct Publishing (KDP) author	Professional seller, vendor, Kindle Direct Publishing (KDP) author	Professional seller, vendor
Product	Adult, used, or refurbished products aren't eligible	Adult, used, or refurbished products aren't eligible	Adult, used, or refurbished products aren't eligible
	Product has to be in stock and in the Buy Box		Product has to be in stock
Brand Registry		Sellers must be enrolled in Amazon Brand Registry	Sellers must be enrolled in Amazon Brand Registry
Categories	Eligible categories	Eligible categories	Eligible categories

.

Is Amazon Pay-Per-Click Advertising a Good Investment?

Amazon PPC campaigns that are well-managed can help you increase sales, boost your organic ranks, and raise your company's profile. Your business may be losing a significant amount of money if you're only using Amazon as a selling platform and not doing any advertising campaigns.

Why should you use Amazon's PPC advertising service?

PPC advertising on Amazon is often more effective than other ad channels since it allows you to target customers where they are most likely to buy (i.e., on Amazon). To get your products in front of as many people as possible, you can use Amazon PPC, which places your advertising on Amazon across mobile and desktop device browsers and the Amazon app. There are a multitude of ad types you can choose from, and you can manage and easily adjust your budget with Amazon PPC. Additionally, you can readily examine how your advertising has fared with a wide range of data.

You can use a variety of targeting tactics, including keywords, ASINs (Amazon Standard Identification Numbers), divisions, companies, and items, as well as outside advertising sites, using Amazon PPC, in order to be sure that your message is being seen by the right people.

How much does Amazon's advertising cost?

An advertiser pays a cost-per-click (CPC) to have their ads appear in the Sponsored Items and Sponsored Brands sections of the search results. The cost per click (CPC) and cost per thousand visible impressions (VCPM) models for promoting display ads exist. You only pay when a prospective customer clicks on your ad with Amazon CPC. If you're willing to spend a certain amount of money per click, you'll be able to control how much you spend on advertising.

How does Amazon's CPC auction function?

A second auction determines the CPC (cost per click) for each ad on Amazon. A baseline bid (the maximum amount an advertiser is prepared to pay for a click) is submitted by each sponsor for their ad. The highest bidder gets the top ad spot (ad rank # 1 and the highest CPC), but they don't pay the whole amount they bid. At Ad Rank Number One, the highest bidder simply has to pay a sliver more than the second-highest bidder to win the bid.

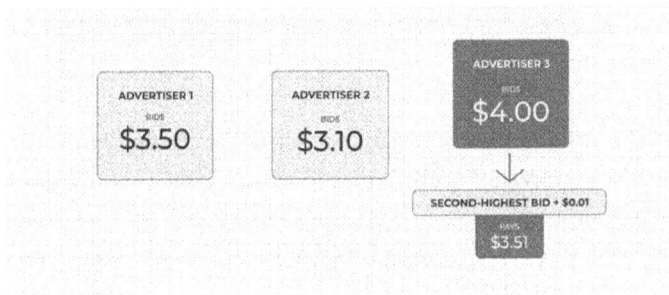

As shown in the preceding example, Sponsor 3 wins the bidding with a $4.00 bid. Advertiser 3 will be charged $3.51 for each click on their ad if it is viewed. As an example, advertiser 1 (ad rank # 2) pays $3.11, and so on for all subsequent ad positions.

What is the average cost per click (CPC) for an Amazon ad campaign?

There is a wide range of CPCs on Amazon.com, ranging from $0.02 to $3.00, although the average CPC can vary substantially depending on product category, marketplace, and ad type.

Are there any additional charges for using Amazon PPC?

The short answer is no. The pricing scheme is clear and simple to understand. As long as you establish your bids and daily PPC budget, you can manage exactly how much money you spend on Amazon advertising. Because of the competitive nature of online advertising, the second-highest bidder in the ad auction determines the precise cost per click. With a winning offer of $0.01 higher than the second-highest, you'll end up paying a total of $0.001.

Is Amazon PPC beneficial for my FBA and FBM products?

Definitely. Product rankings on Amazon are directly affected by Amazon PPC sales, as opposed to Google AdWords. To put it another way, Amazon PPC ads will help your FBA goods rank higher in the organic search results. For new items, this effect is especially essential. Due to a lack of prior sales, new products have a harder time achieving high organic rankings. It is possible to change this through the use of Amazon advertising, which can increase sales and generate reviews for your FBA products.

What You Need to Know About Amazon Advertising Before You Begin

To be effective with Amazon PPC advertising, you must first become familiar with the fundamentals of Amazon advertising. Sellers new to Amazon Sponsored Ads should familiarize themselves with the following terms and concepts:

Building components of Amazon's Pay-Per-Click advertising (basic terminology)

Amazon PPC Key Performance Indicators are extremely useful.

A list of the most critical success factors (KPIs) that will help you gauge the effectiveness of your Amazon advertising is provided below.

The Amazon PPC benchmark tests

·   Where do you need to focus your efforts?

·   What can you do to increase the effectiveness and profitability of your advertising?

When it comes to advertising, the answers to these two questions can be a challenge. The first step to improving your Amazon PPC profile is to see how your KPIs stack up against those of your competitors. Analogies between you and the competitors can only be made using data gathered at the country, category, and ad format levels.

You can use this tool:

·   https://sellics.com/amazon-advertising-benchmark-report/

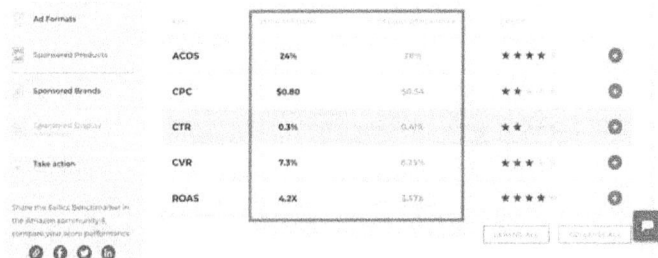

For Amazon ads, what is an acceptable rate of ad click-through?

Products and brands that are promoted on Amazon for three of the most popular categories: Electronics, Clothing, and Health & Household are displayed below.

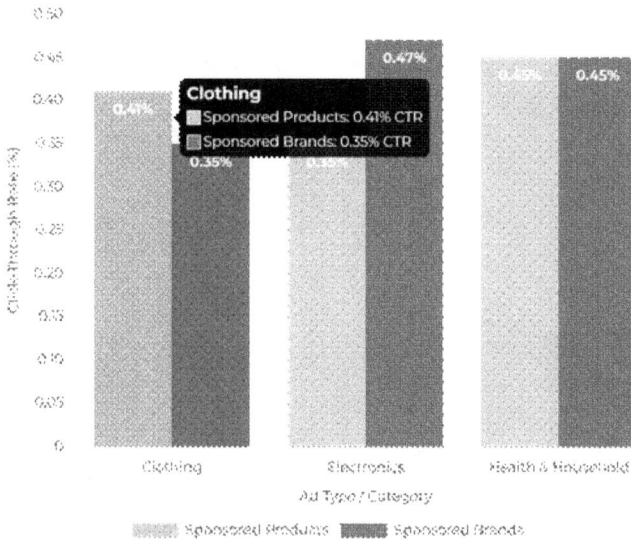

According to this graph, with a 0.40 percent click-through rate for Sponsored brands, you're above the category benchmark and doing well as a clothes retailer. The click-through rate for electronics sellers using Sponsored Brands ads is 0.40 percent, which is significantly lower than the industry average, indicating room for improvement.

This exemplifies an extremely significant point: markets, market segments, and ad formats all have their own unique set of PPC key metrics. Why do you need to make sure you compare your KPIs to your peers? Because this will help identify where your adverts can be improved. By evaluating your click-through rate against that of your competitors, you can determine if there is room for improvement in your product advertisements. Also, comparing your target audience to your peers might help you figure out if you're aiming for too broad or too narrow a demographic.

What is a reasonable Amazon ad conversion rate?

This graph depicts the typical conversion rate for the three most popular ad types.

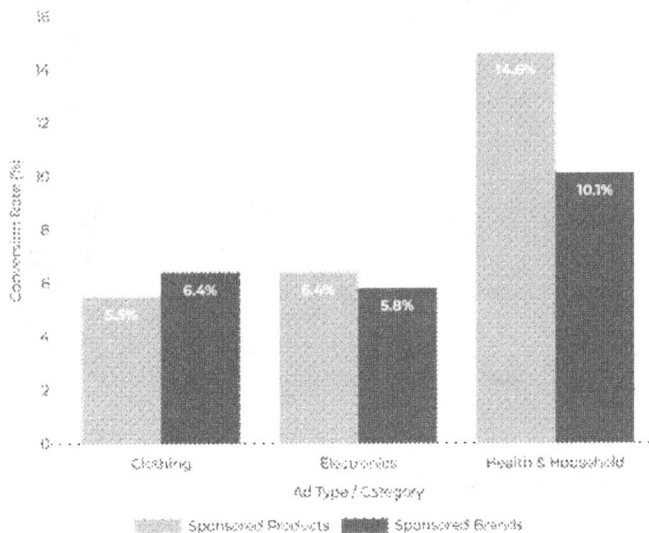

Out of all the categories presented, sponsored products (14.6 percent) and sponsored brands (10.1 percent) had the highest conversion rates in health and household. To put it another way, even within the Health & Household product category, conversion rates vary significantly among advertising forms.

Sponsored products advertisements outperform sponsored brands' ads by a whopping 30.8 percent in this particular category. Your conversion rate can be compared to your peers to see whether there is room for improvement in your landing pages (store, product pages, or product collection pages).

CPC on Amazon: What's an acceptable one?

The average cost per click (CPC) varies by ad type and category.

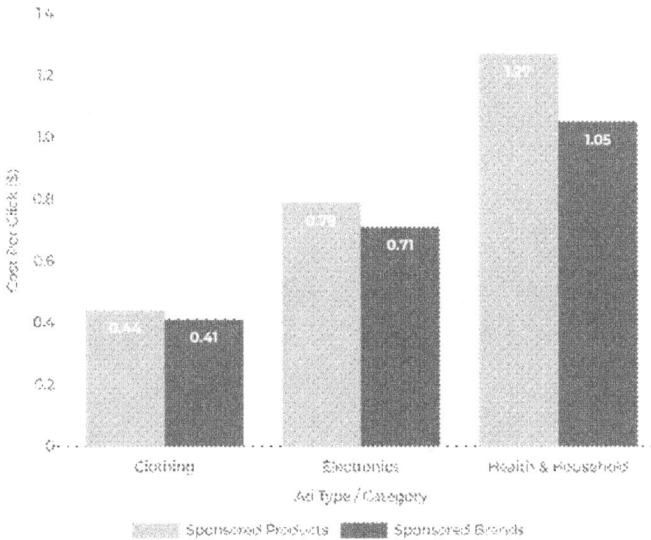

For sponsored brands, click-through costs are typically lower than for sponsored products across all Amazon product categories. The cost per click is a good indicator of the amount of competition in a certain market. As a rule of thumb, if you are spending more per click than your peers, you may be overpaying and hence need to lower your costs. The lower your CPC is compared to your peers, the more likely you are to miss out on potential customers since your bids are not competitive. It's critical to keep in mind that your specific products will determine the best CPC for your campaign. Your budget and your willingness to pay must be taken into consideration.

On Amazon, where can I find a decent ACoS?

For the purposes of comparison, we've included the ACoS for three different sorts of ads: clothing, electronics, and health and household.

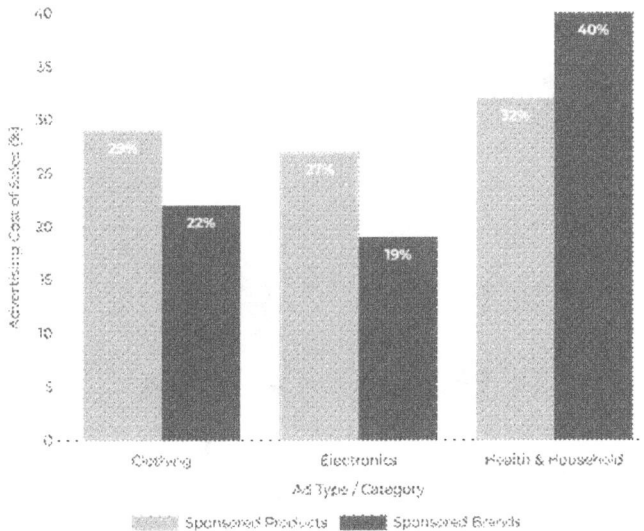

Measurement of Amazon PPC campaigns' efficiency is determined by the ACoS. The ad spend-to-revenue ratio is displayed here. Every dollar spent was matched with a 27-cent investment in Sponsored Products advertising. ACoS comparisons can help you evaluate if your campaigns could be more efficient by optimizing your bids or adding more negative keywords to them. Ad campaign cost-per-click (ACoS) is determined by a variety of factors. Consider your ad goals and your budget when determining your budget and your ability to spend, just like you would with CPCs. Your ad cost per impression (ACoS) should be compared to the ACoS of your competitors in your industry and the marketplace. It's the only way to compare your own performance to that of your competitors.

What you need to know about setting goals for your Amazon ad campaign

If you don't keep tabs on the results of your campaigns in relation to your PPC expenditures, you run the risk of going out of business quickly. Your Amazon PPC campaigns can only be successful if you know exactly what you want them to do before you begin. Typically, you can choose from the following options:

o   Increasing sales, as in the case of a launch date, or increasing impressions, as in the case of a product information campaign. Usually, expenses are maintained at a break-even threshold in this instance, as indicated by the so-called objective KPI "break-even ACoS";

o   Increasing sales while maintaining a predetermined profit margin, as indicated by the so-called target KPI, "target ACoS."

When it comes to Amazon PPC, how much should I be spending?

Calculating your profitability before ad spending (known as "break-even ACoS") is the first step in determining how much you should invest in Amazon ads. Whatever the purpose of your campaign, you must first evaluate your product's profitability to decide how much money you can spend on Amazon PPC advertising.

How can I figure out my profitability and the amount of ACoS needed to break even?

o   Break-Even ACoS = Profit Margin Before Ad Spend

Your profitability before ad spending equals your break-even ACoS. Why? In the example below, your profitability is 25% before advertising costs. You won't lose money if you don't invest more than 25% of your marketing budget on PPC.

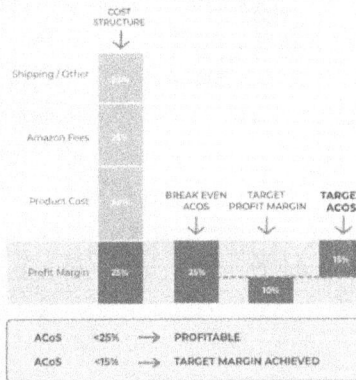

Estimating your break-even ACoS lets you know how much you can spend on PPC without losing money, which is helpful if your campaign's goal is to increase sales or impressions or to raise awareness of your company.

How do I figure out what my ideal ACoS is?

If you want to execute a lucrative promotion, you can utilize your profit margin and break-even ACoS to estimate a reasonable goal profit margin for your item.

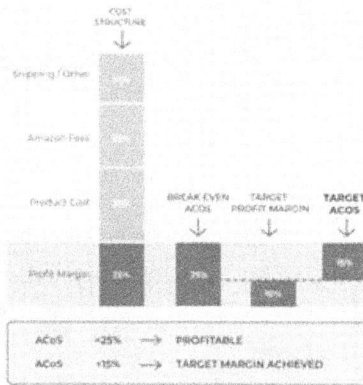

If your break-even ACoS is 25%, and you desire a 10% profit margin after PPC charges, you will have 15% left over to spend on PPC. This is the ACoS you're aiming for. You should never go above your intended ACoS budget in order to ensure that your campaign is lucrative and meets your desired profit margin.

o   Target ACoS = Profit Margin Before Ad Spend – Target Profit Margin After Ad Spend

Start Amazon PPC optimization by optimizing your Amazon listing first.

Before you begin paying for ads on Amazon, you need to ensure that your Amazon product listings are customized for Amazon search engine optimization. In order to target keywords and improve your Amazon PPC advertising conversion rates, Amazon SEO is required.

There are two steps to Amazon SEO:

o   Keyword Optimization: Include as many relevant keywords as possible in the product listing to help it rank well in search results. For both organic and paid advertising, a keyword must be included in your listing in order to generate impressions from ad views and be shown for that term.

o   Listing/Content Optimization: Increase your organic and PPC click-through and lead generation by using high-quality and relevant images, engaging copy, and so on.

Consider the fact that Amazon marketing and Amazon search engine optimization (SEO) work hand in hand. The ad revenue helps your organic rankings as well.

How can Amazon PPC marketing campaigns target specific customers?

Using Amazon PPC, you can reach out to potential buyers in one of four ways. Depending on the ad type, you can choose from a variety of targeting options.

Keywords and match types

Advertisements for sponsored products and sponsored brands can be targeted with keywords. The keywords you use in your ad copy can be based on what shoppers are searching for when they conduct a search. Depending on the search terms used, ads may appear in search results or on product pages that are linked to other sites.

Using the three possible relevant keyword types, you can also fine-tune your advertising placement.

o   Broad match type: Search for words that include all of your keyword's constituent parts, in any combination.

o   Phrase match type: Look for terms that contain all of your keyword parts in the exact same order as you typed them in the search field.

o   Exact match type: Phrases that exactly match your keyword, in the same order and with the same elements.

MATCH TYPE	KEYWORD	AD APPEARS FOR SEARCH TERM	AD DOES NOT APPEAR FOR SEARCH TERM	INCLUDED VARIANTS (MATCHING SEARCH TERMS INCLUDE THE FOLLOWING VARIATIONS)
Broad (search term contains keyword in any word order)	wallet men	wallet men wallet men black nylon wallet men wallet black men men wallet leather	purse men wallet women	- Upper/lowercase (e.g. wallet covers Wallet) - Singular/plural (e.g. wallet covers wallets)
Phrase (search term contains keyword in identical word order)	wallet men	wallet men wallet men black nylon wallet men	purse men wallet women wallet black men men wallet leather	- Special characters (e.g. entrecote covers entrecôte) - Slight spelling errors (e.g. wallet covers welllet)
Exact (Word-for-word match between keyword and search term)	wallet men	wallet men	purse men wallet women wallet men black nylon wallet men wallet black men men wallet leather	- Filler words (e.g. wallets covers for wallet)

There are some subtle differences between comparison types for sponsored brands and other match kinds. Also included in this broad match type are synonyms (such as "wallet" or "purse"). A "+" must be added to a word to signify that it must be maintained without synonyms.

For example, the keyword "+wallet leather" matches with "wallet leather blue" but not with "purse leather blue."

How to conduct a basic search for keywords

You can use this tool:

o   https://sellics.com/sonar-amazon-keyword-tool/

Specification of products (ASINs and categories)

Amazon Product Target marketing (available for all forms of sponsored advertisements) enables you to target your advertising based on the following criteria:

o   Amazon Standard Identification Numbers for products (ASIN)

o   or a category

ASINs are ten-character strings of letters and/or numbers that uniquely identify items for sale on Amazon. The ASIN number can be found on the item's details page. According to the following matrix, there are four common techniques for ASIN targeting:

How to perform basic ASIN research on Amazon

If you're just getting started, you can quickly and easily find ASINs that you can target with your campaign. Look for ASINs that are comparable to yours in the "Products related to this item" section of the Amazon product detail page for your product.

Products related to this item

Examine the "Buyers who saw this product also browsed" section to identify more ASINs to target.

Customers who viewed this item also viewed

Seller and Vendor Central (aka Amazon Retail Analytics) will help you better understand how your customers shop and what products they bundle together.

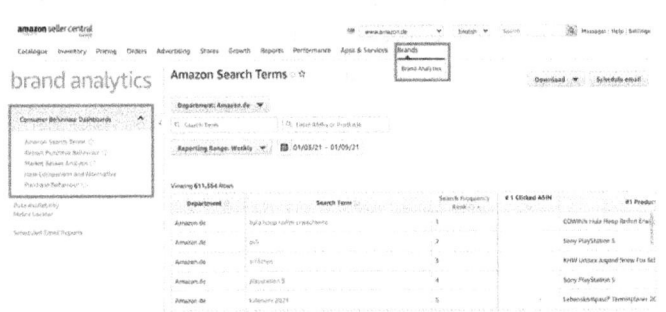

Use the Category Targeting function to narrow your search results by product line in conjunction with ASINs. Targeting works best for the following categories:

o Customers' purchases of innovative brands and items while browsing through categories such as fashion, gifts, and so on;

o This type of targeting increases brand awareness as it generates a large number of impressions quickly and easily.

A lot of people will see and click on your ads if you develop distinct campaigns just for category targeting. Consequently, it tends to require higher costs than other strategies. Separate campaigns are a better option to keep your efforts from running out of money before other targeting approaches obtain enough impressions.

Views remarketing

Remarketing by views is only allowed for sponsored display advertisements. Views Remarketing allows you to reconnect with viewers who have visited your product description and comparable product detail pages but have not purchased your sponsored products within the last 30 days. One substantial variation among views remarketing and other types of marketing is that views remarketing allows you exposure to both on-and off-Amazon placements. With view remarketing, you can attract more customers and retain your merchandise in the minds of people who buy in your field. Your Sponsored Display advertising will also show up on Amazon product detail pages and search engine results pages in addition to off-Amazon locations.

Getting Started with Amazon Pay-Per-Click

Here, we'll go over the basics of getting started with Amazon PPC, including:

1.   Strategy

2.   Setting up a campaign

3.   Optimization of the campaign

Since it's the most profitable ad type, we usually recommend starting with Amazon Sponsored Products first. Sponsored Display and Sponsored Brands can also be used in conjunction with Sponsored Products to contact clients at various points in their customer journey.

An overview of Amazon's ad formats

Here are a few examples of each of the three Amazon ad formats:

Amazon Sponsored Products: A Beginner's Guide

Your sponsored product campaign should be structured in the following manner.

The following is a beginner's guide to a sponsored product strategy. Each product or collection of products has a suggested plan and structure. Use products with similar keywords and profitability if you're using a group of them. There are two campaigns in the strategy:

- 1 **automatic** campaign (with 1 automatic ad group)
- 1 **manual** campaign (with 1 ad group for **broad** match keywords and 1 ad group for **ASIN** targets

As a general rule, you should be using your automatic campaign to conduct constant target research while regularly transferring high-performing keywords and ASINs to your manual campaign, where they can be fine-tuned for the best possible results. Automated campaigns (low effort) and manual campaigns (high precision) can both benefit from this technique.

Sponsored Products Getting Started Strategy

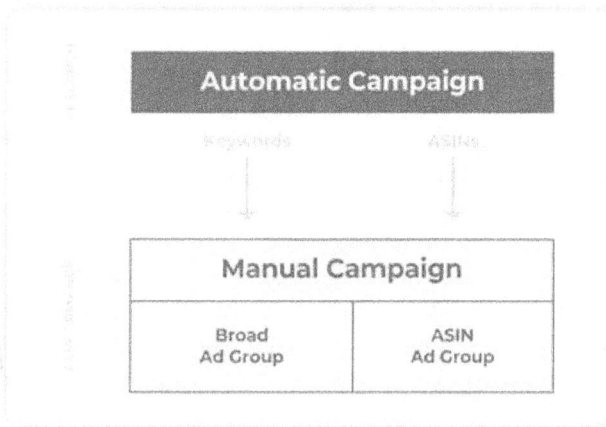

Automatic Campaign	
Keywords	ASINs

Manual Campaign	
Broad Ad Group	ASIN Ad Group

You can also use your automated Sponsored Products campaign to move well-performing keywords and ASINs to your sponsored brands and paid display campaigns.

Assembling a Sponsored Product Campaign

Automated campaigns are simple to set up. There are only a few things to do: choose a campaign name, budget, and CPC bid. As soon as your campaign is up and running, Amazon begins scanning the sponsored products and displaying your adverts for Amazon-selected search phrases. This is a good place to begin. Adding your own beginning keywords requires the creation of a manual campaign. Research about 20 keywords and put them in your "Broad" ad group for a good amount of coverage. Your campaign should additionally include an ASIN ad group of about 20 ASINs. Take a look at your branded analytics tool, the "Products similar to this item" area, or the "Clients who viewed this item also visited" section on the Amazon detail page for your item to determine which first ASINs to add to your manual group. An overview of all the options can be seen in the table that follows:

SETTINGS	AUTOMATIC	MANUAL (BROAD KEYWORDS)	MANUAL (ASIN)
Budget	$15 per product	$25 per product	
Campaign name	SP | 'Fill in ASIN' | Auto	SP | 'Fill in ASIN' | Manual	
Ad group name	SP | 'Fill in ASIN' | Auto	SP | 'Fill in ASIN' | Manual | KW Broad	SP | 'Fill in ASIN' | Manual | ASIN
Products	Product or product set with similar keywords and margins	Product or product set with similar keywords and margins	Product or product set with similar keywords and margins
Initial Targets	None	Around 20 broad keywords	Around 20 ASINs
Initial Negative Targets	Initial targets from 'Broad' ad group (as negative phrase) and from 'ASIN' ad group	None	None
Ad group bid	Suggested bid by Amazon		
Target bid			

Impression generation is limited to the specific ad groups we specify using negative targeting. Why? Campaigns that are run manually or automatically can both target specific keywords and ASINs. This means that all impressions from the automatic campaign must be stopped as soon as a target is added to the manual campaign so that the manual campaign may better target this target. A negative phrase keyword or ASIN must be added to the manual campaign whenever the target is added to stop impressions from being sent out automatically. A target should be harvested and moved from automated to manual harvesting when campaigns are started or created.

Maximizing the effectiveness of your sponsored products

With Amazon advertising, standard campaign improvement is the key to success. However, once you've gathered enough data (impressions, clicks, conversions, etc.) to analyze your current campaign effectiveness, you'll want to make improvements to your PPC campaigns. If you have adequate data, there are three optimization procedures you should apply on a regular basis:

1.   Transfer keywords and ASINs from an auto-campaign to a manual campaign.

The broad match and ASIN ad groups in your manual campaign are where you'll be able to fine-tune your top-performing search terms (keywords and ASINs) over time.

To use an example:

o   The auto campaign identifies the suitable search keyword as "wallet blue."

o   The keyword "wallet blue" is placed in the manual broad match ad group in order to maximize the keyword bid there.

o   Simultaneously, the negative phrase keyword "wallet blue" must be included in the automated campaign, preventing views for this search term.

2.   Use negative keywords

The search queries (keywords and ASINs) that are producing clicks but no sales in your auto campaign and manual campaign should be tracked regularly and added as negative keywords/ASINs to prevent unwanted PPC expenditures from building up.

If your Amazon marketing campaigns and ad groups aren't successful, you want to eliminate:

o   Search phrases that are blatantly unrelated to your product's description.

o   Money-losing search Keywords that may be relevant to your goods but which merely produce clicks and not conversions on your site.

Negative keywords can help you lower your ACoS if you use them effectively.

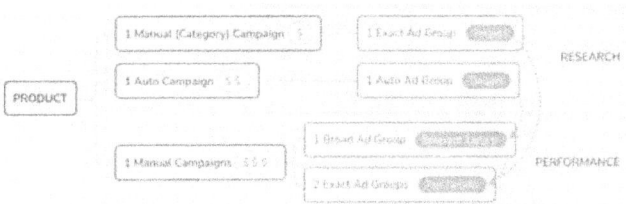

3.   Optimize the bids on your Amazon CPC advertisements

Before you can identify the best CPC, ad groups, ASINs, and keywords should have a clear purpose, and ACoS target values should be defined.

Goal is maximizing sales or impressions:
ACoS target value = break-even ACoS = profit margin before ad spend

Goal is achieving target profit margin after ad spend:
ACoS target value = target ACoS = profit margin before ad spend – profit margin after ad spend

Test several CPCs to discover which one is closest to your aim once you have specified your goal and targets. Standard logical rules for optimizing your CPC bids include the following:

Keywords / ASINs with good ACoS:
IF ACoS < Target value, THEN increase target bid

Keywords / ASINs with poor ACoS:
IF ACoS > Target value, THEN decrease target bid

Keywords / ASINs without conversions:
Reduce bid or pause

Keywords with few or no impressions:
Keywords that receive little or no impressions:

Make sure the term is included in your product description if you don't see any views. Increase the bid on keywords and ASINs if there aren't many impressions for your product.

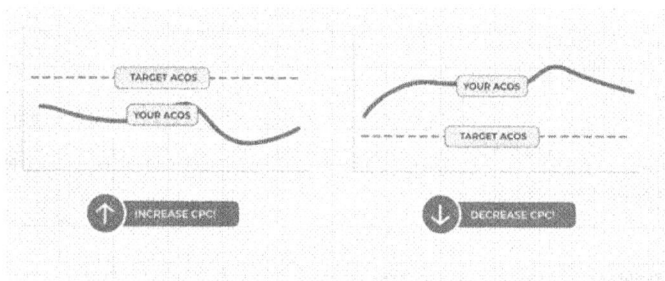

It's crucial to provide enough time between keyword and ASIN bid revisions, so keep that in mind. Your bid modifications should only be made once you've gathered enough data to determine whether or not they're essential.

First steps with Sponsored Brands

Prior to launching an advertising campaign, it's crucial to know what your goals are: are you trying to enhance brand awareness, increase revenue, or recruit new customers? The number of impressions (ad views) your advertising receives is critical if you want to boost your brand's visibility. Keep an eye on your ad's conversion rate and cost per click (CPC) if you want to increase sales, bearing in mind that the "Top of Search" location is costlier than "Other Placements." There are several ways to assess if you have a customer acquisition objective, and one of the most effective is Amazon's new-to-brand analytics.

Targeted Brands Campaign Setup

To get started, gather together three of your best-selling products that share the same keyword. You'll be putting these three things together in a banner, so choose well and make sure they all work well together. The best-performing keywords from your sponsored product campaigns should be used to construct a sponsored brand product collection campaign for each product grouping.

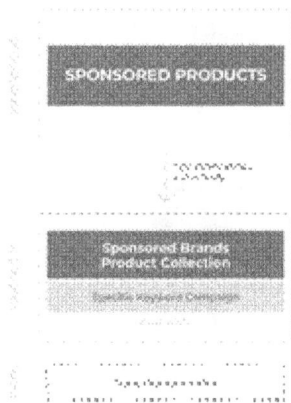

Best Practices for Sponsored Brands

When creating Promoted Brands campaigns, the following are the primary standard procedures to follow:

o   Spend on a high-quality lifestyle photograph that accurately portrays your goods.

o   Spend some time crafting a clickable headline. Be inventive! Consider what your customers appreciate most about your product. Of course, ensure that you've covered the essentials.

§ Make use of sentence case.

§ Maintain relevance.

§ Consider inserting a call to action.

§ However, avoid adding pressure: emotive language such as "don't wait, buy now!" is banned.

§ When in doubt, provide a description of the product.

o   Experiment with the selection and arrangement of products. If you have a single flagship product, consider showcasing it in related groupings to draw attention to the collection.

o   If you have a brand store, consider linking to it to boost your ROAS. Keep in mind that you may also use sub-pages for greater specificity.

o   Maintain an eye on your inventory. Because your advertisements will continue to run even if you are out of stock of one of the top picks, they should be manually stopped.

o   Begin by focusing on specialized or long-tail product keywords that can help you achieve your productivity (sales and profit) goals.

Before you start tweaking your Sponsored Brands advertising, you'll want to ensure that you've gathered sufficient data (impressions, clicks, and sales, for example).

Your Sponsored Brands campaign should include both branded and non-branded keywords.

Keyword research is critical for Sponsored Brands campaigns, just as it is for those promoting Sponsored Products. Search engines display ads only when one of your keywords is relevant to the shopper's query. The keywords you choose should be applicable to each of the three products you're promoting at the same time.

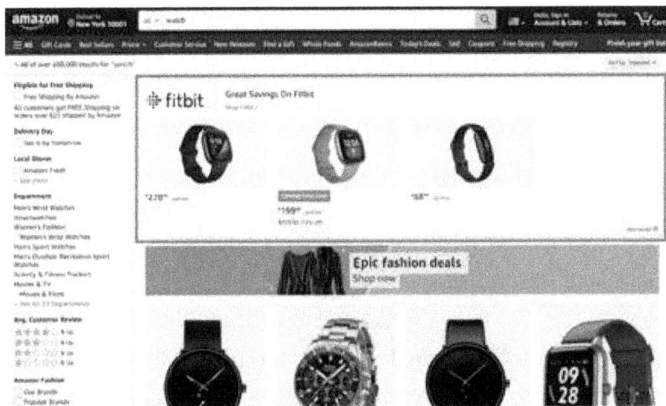

If your goal is to raise awareness of your brand, you should use generic, non-branded keywords and highlight your best-selling items to draw in customers who are just learning about your company. If you have a well-established brand, establish a special brand protection campaign and concentrate on your brand's keywords. Protecting your portion of the market in this way is beneficial.

Automatic Promoted Items campaign keyword collection and analysis

The recommended strategy is to extract the highest keywords from your automatic sponsored product campaigns if you have sponsored product ads running for the products listed in your Amazon Sponsored Brands campaign. Go to the "search terms" tab in your automated Sponsored Products campaign in Seller Central to identify these keywords.

Placement analysis of sponsored brands

Your Amazon Sponsored Brands ad placements should be evaluated once your campaign is up and running. Sponsored Brands "Keyword Placement" and "Campaign Placement" reports allow you to go further into the specifics of your placement efforts.

Campaign type   ○ Sponsored Products
                 ● Sponsored Brands
                 ○ Sponsored Brands video
                 ○ Sponsored Display ⊕ **New**

Report type ⊕ | Keyword

Time unit | Keyword placement ᶠ

                 | Campaign

Report period | Campaign placement

                 | Search term

As a result of this, Amazon does not discriminate between "Other Placements" and "Other Search Placements," which include both search results and product pages. This means that only your "Top of Search" placement can be compared to your "Other Placements" in terms of performance. Amazon's auto bidding function can be disabled if you notice that a certain ad's click-through and conversion rates are not in line with your PPC goals.

Is it better to use pre-set bid modifications or create my own?

For all of your Sponsored Brands initiatives, Amazon uses an automatic bidding system. You can utilize the custom bid adjustment feature to lower your bid percentage for a certain placement category if the click-through rate and accompanying sales are exceptionally low.

Product targeting and bids ⊕

Default bid ⊕
1.00   €

Automated bidding ⊕
☐ Allow Amazon to automatically optimise bids for placements other than top of search.

☑ Set a custom bid adjustment
Decrease by ∨   30 % for placements other than top of search
For example: a 60% decrease on a 5.00 € bid will become 3.00 €

First steps with Sponsored Display

If a customer has viewed a specific product detail page, you can use Amazon Sponsored Display advertisements to target them both on and off Amazon. Sales are increased by sponsored display advertising since it retargets clients who have already shown an interest in your goods. "Retail aware" advertisements are another benefit of sponsored display ads. They only appear if your products are available for immediate purchase or if you have a featured offer.

Using remarketing solutions like Sponsored Display, you can exclude clients who have already purchased the items you're trying to sell. For Sponsored Display advertisements, you can either pay per click (CPC) or per 1,000 visible impressions, depending on your preference. Sellers registered with Amazon's brand registry can use sponsored display ads, as can vendors. Sponsored Display advertising offers two types of targeting options: product targeting and view remarketing.

Specification of products (ASIN or category)

Sponsored Display advertisements can be displayed based on ASIN or category targeting.

o   On the product detail pages of Amazon

o   On PC, mobile, and the Amazon app, in search results

o   On Amazon's main page

The following is an illustration of a sponsored display ad that appears on a product detail page. You can use this form of sponsored display ad below the "Add to Cart" button to draw visitors away from competitors and persuade your potential customers to buy more than one product from you.

Sponsored display ads can also be used to advertise comparable products. Your advertisement will show up when someone is considering purchasing a PS4 and your PS4 ASIN can be used to promote a carrying case.

This increases the possibility of a customer adding your goods to their shopping cart because it informs them that a complementary product is available that they may like or need.

Views remarketing

Customers who have recently viewed your product's detail page or comparable product and category detail pages can be retargeted with view remarketing. It is possible to show your adverts on third-party websites and apps in addition to the places on Amazon, such as product detail pages and search results. The likelihood of a sale is higher because the potential consumer has previously shown an interest in the category in which your product falls. Views remarketing is a great strategy for building brand awareness and keeping your goods in the minds of potential buyers, even if the visitor does not make an early purchase.

Preparation of your sponsored advertisement display

Use merchandise targeting for aggressive ASIN targets in your first sponsored display campaign. For offensive ASIN targets, focus on products that your rivals are selling as a substitute or as a complementary offering.

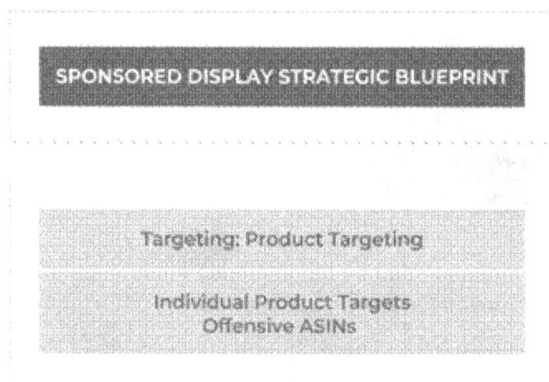

SPONSORED DISPLAY STRATEGIC BLUEPRINT

Targeting: Product Targeting

Individual Product Targets
Offensive ASINs

Try searching the Amazon search bar for some of the keywords in your product descriptions to see who else is selling similar products. If you choose aggressive ASIN targets, you'll be able to take advantage of the product detail page traffic of your competitors and/or take their clients.

Conclusion

Amazon FBA is the logical solution if you don't have a specialized logistics crew, delivery vans, or a warehouse where you can store your products. Just imagine how much more challenging it will be if you are also in charge of the company's order fulfillment in addition to selling and marketing. Amazon FBA, on the other hand, is a godsend for both new and experienced sellers alike. Amazon Prime, was launched in February 2005 as part of the company's "all-you-can-eat" quick shipping program.

The major goal of the aforementioned customer loyalty program is to recruit more consumers and increase sales volume. It was easy to lure in online consumers since, after all, who wouldn't want to receive their orders in less than two days? It takes around 4-5 days for normal delivery to arrive. Furthermore, you only have to pay a significant one-time price (at first, it was $79 per year) to use the service for a year. In comparison to paying a small fee ($9.48 at the time) for two-day delivery on every order, this is more cost-effective in the long run. Amazon understands that continuing to bear the burden of shipping and logistics costs will have a negative impact on their bottom line as more online buyers join the Prime program. As a result, in 2006, Amazon FBA was established.

When Amazon established its Fulfillment by Amazon (FBA) service in 2006, the goal was to streamline operations that would benefit both the company's merchants and its customers. Because of its widespread popularity, it has grown into an extremely useful tool that helps businesses overcome fulfillment and customer service difficulties while also offering access to a comprehensive fulfillment network. The goal was to connect Amazon's existing fulfillment strategy with third-party seller operations in order to benefit from this infrastructure.

Not only would vendors stand to benefit greatly from the introduction of this service, but their customers would also benefit from receiving faster, more dependable shipping and service from this marketplace behemoth. How Fulfillment by Amazon works is as follows: you sell the item, and Amazon ships it to the buyer. Your deliveries will be taken care of by the eCommerce shipping and logistics team. If you want to kill two birds with one stone, consider enrolling in Amazon FBA, which will allow you to start selling and building your online retail business almost immediately. Simply follow the methods outlined in this guide and avoid making the mistakes listed above to maintain your excellent standing with Amazon.

www.ingramcontent.com/pod-product-compliance
Lightning Source LLC
Chambersburg PA
CBHW071331210326
41597CB00015B/1417